Happiness: A Very Short Introduction

VERY SHORT INTRODUCTIONS are for anyone wanting a stimulating and accessible way in to a new subject. They are written by experts, and have been published in more than 25 languages worldwide.

The series began in 1995, and now represents a wide variety of topics in history, philosophy, religion, science, and the humanities. The VSI Library now contains more than 300 volumes—a Very Short Introduction to everything from ancient Egypt and Indian philosophy to conceptual art and cosmology—and will continue to grow in a variety of disciplines.

Very Short Introductions available now:

Available soon:

THE PALESTINIAN-ISRAELI
  CONFLICT Martin Bunton
MANAGEMENT John Hendry

FOOD John Krebs
MODERN WAR Richard English
SOCIOLINGUISTICS John Edwards

For more information visit our website
www.oup.com/vsi/

Daniel M. Haybron

HAPPINESS

A Very Short Introduction

OXFORD
UNIVERSITY PRESS

OXFORD
UNIVERSITY PRESS

Great Clarendon Street, Oxford, ox2 6DP,
United Kingdom

Oxford University Press is a department of the University of Oxford.
It furthers the University's objective of excellence in research, scholarship,
and education by publishing worldwide. Oxford is a registered trade mark of
Oxford University Press in the UK and in certain other countries

First Edition published in 2013

Impression: 1

British Library Cataloguing in Publication Data

Data available

ISBN 978-0-19-959060-5

Printed in Great Britain by
Ashford Colour Press Ltd, Gosport, Hampshire

For Elizabeth

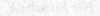

Contents

Contents

Acknowledgements

For their invaluable assistance with this book, I am most grateful to
Andrea Keegan, Anna Alexandrova, Anne Margaret Baxley, Antti
Kauppinen, Barbara Baumgartner, Boyce Nute, Carol and Joel
Friedman, Chad Flanders, Charlie Kurth, David Brax, David
Chalmers, David Haybron, Deborah Welch, Elizabeth Foreman,
Emma Ma, Eric Brown, Eric Wiland, Erik Angner, Gerardo Camilo,
Jason Raibley, John Brunero, John Doris, Jona Ross, Julia
Annas, Julia Driver, Lori Lipkind, Neil Thin, Paul Dolan, Robert
Biswas-Diener, Robert Sullivan, robert wolff, Sara Bernal, Scott
Berman, Scott Ragland, Sean Davies, Troy DeArmitt, Valerie
Tiberius, and anonymous reviewers for Oxford University Press. For
support in writing this book, I want to thank my department chair,
Fr. Theodore Vitali, and Saint Louis University. For their support
and mentorship in these matters over the years, I wish to thank
Douglas Husak, Stephen Stich, and L. W. Sumner, whose pioneering
philosophical work on happiness made my own researches possible.
I owe a special debt to Ed Diener, who more or less invented the
contemporary field of happiness research, and has contributed more
to the study of happiness than anyone living. His own life pretty well
embodies what this book is about, which is not to say he'll agree with
everything in it. (We scholars get paid to disagree, after all.) There
are few academics I admire, as a scholar or a person, as much as Ed.

Above all, I want to thank my most patient and incisive reader and
advisor, my wife Elizabeth.

List of illustrations

The publisher and the author apologize for any errors or omissions in the above list. If contacted they will be happy to rectify these at the earliest opportunity.

Chapter 1
A remarkable fact

I have been wondering at your peaceful slumbers, and that was the reason why I did not awaken you, because I wanted you to be out of pain. I have always thought you happy in the calmness of your temperament; but never did I see the like of the easy, cheerful way in which you bear this calamity.

> Crito to Socrates, who awaits execution. From Plato, *Crito*

I asked the Pirahãs once during my early missionary years if they knew why I was there. 'You are here because this is a beautiful place. The water is pretty. There are good things to eat here. The Pirahãs are nice people.' That was and is the Pirahãs' perspective. Life is good. Their upbringing, everyone learning early on to pull their own weight, produces a society of satisfied members. That is hard to argue against.

> Daniel Everett, *Don't Sleep, There Are Snakes*

Happiness in unexpected places

In all of human history, there may never have been a better time to be alive. In fact economist Charles Kenny declared the period 2000–10 to be the 'best decade ever'. Even with the wars raging in various parts of the globe, people are less likely than ever to die at the hands of others. We can expect to live *decades* longer than any generation until the last century. Worldwide, the average life expectancy is 68 years, more than double what it was in 1900. Dire poverty and many forms of oppression are on the decline. And you and I enjoy a material and cultural abundance undreamt of for the vast majority of human history. We are, by historical standards, *rich*.

So lucky are we that we can easily come to believe that those without such abundance must be miserable. Or, at least, far less happy than we.

This thought is not obviously true. Consider the Greek thinker Socrates. Yes, he more or less invented philosophy, and Western civilization while he was at it. But he also didn't have television, a dishwasher, a furnace, air conditioning, a fan, a phone, or a clock. No Mister Steamy Dryer Balls, no Xbox, no iPod, iPad, or iAnything. Socrates inhabited what we would now call a 'lesser-developed' town called Athens, where no one had any of these things. There wasn't even a World Bank to build them a dam. The wealthiest Athenians did have slaves, which was probably a plus (for them, not the slaves).

But in material terms they were, by today's standards, poor. No refrigerator, no toilet, no toilet paper, no antibiotics, and no decent anaesthetics. In the evenings there was nothing to do, so you had no choice but to talk to other people. And drink wine, and eat Greek food. Sing a few songs, tell a few jokes. Look up at the starry sky. And test theories regarding the best sort of partner for exploring the pleasures of the flesh (see Plato, *Symposium*). On the bright side, Socrates did manage to grow old. But for drinking from the poison cup of hemlock, he would have grown even older.

What, no tears for Socrates? Perhaps you were under the impression that he was actually rather happy. Indeed, that is the standard story. Socrates' indefatigable good cheer and equanimity, even in the face of death, were legendary, and just about all the major philosophical schools that followed held him up as a paradigm of the happy, flourishing man. Many things have been said of Socrates, but 'pitiable' is not one of them. He had, by all indications, what even today's comfortable reader will recognize as a great life. Socrates didn't miss out on a thing.

Fast-forward a couple of thousand years. A team of psychologists ventures out to study well-being among three traditional, small-scale societies: the Amish, the Maasai, and the Inughuit. The Amish live in traditional farming communities in a manner much like that of a couple of hundred years ago, though they are happy to embrace new technologies that do not threaten their values of community and humility. The Maasai are herders whose members live in huts made of excrement, and whose men are expected to kill a lion with a spear if they really wish to prove their manhood. The Inughuit lead a hunter-gatherer lifestyle in Greenland, which is probably one of the less appealing places to be a hunter-gatherer.

The researchers applied a battery of measures of happiness and life satisfaction in each of these societies, including measures of positive and negative emotions. (No small job, that: to get the Maasai even to talk to these contemptible city-slickers, the lead investigator found it necessary to volunteer for a very, very painful scarification ritual, which essentially involves having pieces of your chest burned off, muscle and all, with a hot stick. If you so much as make a sound, you're a wimp.) Table 1 shows how they did compared to some other groups, looking just at self-reported satisfaction with their lives.

Measures of positive versus negative emotions also were quite favourable for all three groups, particularly the high-spirited Maasai. Many would take the results to show that these 'poor' communities are all happier than the average *college student*, and in two cases just as happy as the richest Americans. This would be an over-hasty conclusion, as we'll see. But if life is just a vale of tears for these folks, they've apparently not figured it out.

Table 1 Life satisfaction of various groups

Positive groups	LS
Forbes richest Americans	5.8
Pennsylvania Amish	5.8
Inughuit (Inuit group from Northern Greenland)	5.8
East African Maasai	5.4
International college students (47 nations)	4.9
Calcutta slum dwellers	4.6
Neutral point of scale = 4.0	
Groups below neutral	**LS**
Calcutta sex workers	3.6
Calcutta homeless	3.2
California homeless	2.9

Notes: LS scores are based on responses to the statement 'You are satisfied with your life', on a 7-point scale from 1 (*strongly disagree*) to 7 (*strongly agree*).

Similar results abound in cross-cultural studies of well-being, to the point that one recent scholarly tome on global trends in happiness was subtitled, 'the paradox of happy peasants and miserable millionaires'. To date the best international study of human well-being, the Gallup World Poll, has surveyed over 136,000 people in 155 countries, using a rich set of measures of life satisfaction, emotional experience, and other points of experienced quality of life. The happiest nation? By one life satisfaction measure, Denmark, which has had a habit of hogging the top spot in these kinds of studies.

In terms of daily experience—roughly, how pleasant or emotionally rewarding life is—top honours went to...Panama. On that measure the United States placed 57th. In life satisfaction, it ranked a more respectable 14th.

Costa Rica, which is poor but has no army, a healthy democracy, universal healthcare, and comparable life expectancy to the United States, ranked fifth on the planet in daily experience, sixth in life satisfaction. (For what it's worth, I recently asked a young woman who had spent some time living in Costa Rica whether such findings gibed with her experience. She seemed to think me daft even to pose the question—'Of *course*. Everybody's happy there.') The only affluent countries to beat Costa Rica on either measure were the Netherlands and the Nordic countries. These results are not unusual.

You might wonder how reliable such studies are, a question we'll take up later. But personal observation of such populations, by happiness researchers and many other people, suggests that the numbers have some plausibility. Looking to the extreme end of the material spectrum, consider a recent account by linguist Daniel Everett. His book, *Don't Sleep, There Are Snakes*, describes the Pirahã (pronounced 'pee-da-han'), a hunter-gatherer people with whom he lived for many years in the Amazon. Their way of life is bare-bones even by hunter-gatherer standards, and yet:

> I have never heard a Pirahã say that he or she is worried. In fact, as far as I can tell, the Pirahãs have no word for *worry* in their language. One group of visitors to the Pirahãs, psychologists from the Massachusetts Institute of Technology's Brain and Cognitive Science Department, commented that the Pirahãs appeared to be the happiest people they had ever seen. I asked them how they could test such a statement. They replied that one way might be to measure the time that the average Pirahã spends smiling and laughing and then to compare this with the number of minutes members of other societies, such as Americans, spend smiling and laughing. They suggested that the Pirahãs would win hands down.

This is just one of many written accounts of a similar nature. Another researcher has related to me in some detail his experience working with a hunter-gatherer tribe whose members quite enjoy the way they live, and whom he regards as having a very good quality of life. Some of them have left the tribe, met with success in our world, and returned nevertheless to their old lives in the jungle. This likely owed partly to a 'fish out of water' experience that anyone might have in a strange land and partly to discrimination they faced in our world. But they also, simply, preferred their own way of life, and the tribe has refused offers to increase their material standard of living. Their happiness is not simply a product of ignorance about the wonders of plasma TV. They know about such things, but don't much care.

A note of caution is in order. There is a long and dismal tradition of painting indigenous peoples as leading idealized,

1. Maasai women

6

idyllic lives—in effect reducing them to props in our own fantasies. Perhaps to distance themselves from this patronizing nonsense, commentators can go to some lengths to portray such peoples as vicious or pathetic, or take care never to put in a positive word about their way of life. This too is noxious rubbish, but I will not try to rebut it here. Interested readers can consult the literature and form their own judgements on this question.

But let's dispatch the romanticism: everybody has problems. However happy some hunters might be, they still have shorter lives and lose many of their children. I've been told, of more than one indigenous people, that they envied nothing in Western civilization but the healthcare. But that is actually quite a lot. Without it, I would not be writing this. If you read Everett's full account of the Pirahã, his claims about happiness are liable to seem reasonable, but he makes clear that their lives are hardly perfect. (Average life expectancy: around 45 years.)

It cannot be stated too emphatically that many poor people are by no means flourishing. Worldwide, poverty is a tremendous source of unhappiness. Regarding hunter-gatherer cultures, Everett himself notes that 'many others, if not all, that I have studied are often sullen and withdrawn, torn between the desire to maintain their cultural autonomy and to acquire the goods of the outside world'.

But then he adds, 'The Pirahãs have no such conflicts'. They like our stuff, but don't really want the aggravation that goes with getting it. Elsewhere, he relates his experience telling the Pirahãs the tragic tale of his stepmother's suicide. They crack up. It's not that they are mean: to them it is incomprehensibly, hilariously bizarre that anybody would do such a thing. They know plenty about pain—but not, apparently, the kind of searing, isolating spiritual agony that would drive someone to take her own life.

The world is a big place, with many kinds of poverty, or more accurately unaffluence. We should beware of simple generalizations about large swathes of humanity. From the observation that some peoples with meagre possessions seem happy, or unhappy, we should not assume that all such peoples are.

But here's the thing: from the conventional viewpoint of modern civilization, the mere fact that *any* population could have such limited means, living at the zero point of what we call development, and give the appearance of doing pretty well, if not better than many of us rich folks, is absolutely remarkable. *It only takes one community like that, or even a Socrates, to raise some fairly profound questions*. And these are among the most basic questions that any civilized society must come to grips with. How is it possible to have so little, yet lead a rich and fulfilling life? Indeed, to be happy? What is happiness, anyway, and what really matters in life? What should our priorities be?

Consider your own case. You are, let us suppose, on your deathbed. What from your life would you most like to have just one more experience of? What would you most regret leaving behind? I can already tell you the first thing you'll want to say, if you're even remotely normal: more time with your loved ones. I would wager that, for most people in just about every corner of the world, that answer will simply dwarf all other contenders. What else, then? Here people are likely to begin parting ways, though I suspect that high on most lists would be such experiences as these: another sunset, another look at greenery or the ocean, a chance to hear the birds sing once more.

What most certainly will not be on the list: another peck at the mobile phone, or one more trip to the mall. How about an extra day at the office?

Time is the currency of life, and a poor person of 70 years has no less of it than a rich person. If you can spend much of that time in the company of people you love and taking in the wonders of a spectacularly beautiful planet, you've already got a lot going for you. If, to boot, you've got some interesting things to do, and aren't in too much physical or emotional pain, you might be just about there.

You don't have to be rich to enjoy these things, and plenty of materially poor people have all of them. Yes, money can help. But lots of rich people lack all of these things—mired in their own kind of poverty—and are miserable. The essentials of a good life are available even to people who don't own much—and even, we will see, to those who never manage to be happy. I would venture that most people experience enough love, enough beauty, and not so much pain, that they can honestly say that their lives are good. Go back and look at the life satisfaction numbers for the slum dwellers of Calcutta, also known as the City of Joy: positive. Life is hard, yes. But it is also, for most, good.

Defining happiness

We need to get clearer on what we mean by happiness. You might wonder whether the whole business of defining happiness makes much sense. After all, more than a few people have suggested that happiness cannot be defined. The word has too many meanings, or is too obscure: a blank canvas on which to hang our longings. So trying to give a theory of happiness is just tilting at windmills.

But is it really? I don't think so. The first thing to do is give up the idea that any single account of happiness can capture everything we use the word to talk about. But the fact remains that we use it to talk about certain sorts of things we care about. So we can ask why we *care* about happiness, and whether some proposed definition makes sense of our practical concerns. One sign of an unhelpful definition of happiness is that it leaves mysterious why anyone should care about it.

In a nutshell, we can *reconstruct* the ordinary notion of happiness, taking the formless blob of everyday happiness talk and sharpening it into a form that helps us to think clearly about matters of importance. Instead of saying, unequivocally, that 'happiness is x', we should say that 'happiness is usefully thought of as x'.

The alternative? Silence. Stop trying to figure out whether people are right to care so much about happiness. Don't bother asking whether our way of life promotes or frustrates happiness. Worry not about whether your children are unhappy, or whether your divorce will actually make them happier, as you'd like to think. For none of these questions has any discernible meaning, and their import is completely up in the air.

We could do that. But it seems like a pretty foolish thing to do. 'Happiness' is a central term in our everyday vocabularies, and people use it all the time to think and talk about things they care about. Real concerns, real problems. It behooves those of us who get paid to study such things to help people think more clearly and intelligently about those concerns. And for that we need to figure out what the important things are that people use 'happiness' to talk about. We need a theory—a definition—of happiness. The word itself isn't important. It's the things we use it to talk about that matter.

In this book, 'happiness' is nothing more than a word for a certain state of mind. We will be asking, then, what that state of mind is; what brings it; and how important it is in a good life.

Some readers may be disappointed to hear that happiness is nothing more than a psychological condition. Isn't there more to life than that? Indeed there is, as most philosophers see things, myself included. Happiness is awfully important, but probably not the only thing that matters. This too may seem a bit deflating to some: perhaps you thought happiness was, pretty much by *definition*, the measure of a good life. Maybe you picked up this book with precisely that question in mind: you wanted to know about a lot more than just some state of mind. You wanted to read about what really matters in life. In which case you might be wondering if it's time for a refund.

We will get to the big questions in due course. Happiness, the state of mind, has such a grip on the popular imagination that a proper appreciation of its pursuit requires us to set it in the context of what, in general, matters for a good life.

While this book is about happiness, the state of mind, other books sometimes use the word for a value notion, *well-being*: a life that goes well for you. When the ancient Greek philosopher Aristotle (384–322 BCE) said something about 'happiness'—his word was *eudaimonia*—he was talking about the value notion. And his concern was not to understand a state of mind. He wanted to know what sort of life ultimately benefits a person, serves her interests, or makes her better off. Suppose a man leads a pleasant life of utter passivity, living like a pig and letting his potential go to waste. Can he really be doing well? This is a question of values, not psychology. To avoid confusion, I'll use the word 'well-being' when talking about what benefits a person, and save 'happiness' for the psychological notion.

So we've narrowed our focus to happiness as a psychological matter. With that in mind, we can identify three basic theories about what happiness is:

1. Emotional state theory: happiness as a positive emotional condition
2. Hedonism: happiness as pleasure
3. Life satisfaction theory: happiness as being satisfied with your life

Very roughly, the first two theories think of happiness in terms of *feelings*, while the life satisfaction theory sees happiness mainly as a *judgement* about one's life. The differences between these views will become clearer over the next two chapters.

Psychologists studying 'happiness' often talk about it in terms of *subjective well-being*, which has two parts: life satisfaction and a positive emotional condition. In essence, subjective well-being views of happiness combine theories 1 and 3 from our list. I will set this sort of view aside, as I think it unhelpfully lumps together two very different things. Subjective well-being is better understood as a catch-all term for the psychological aspects of well-being, not a synonym for happiness.

About the book

Ultimately, this book is about happiness in both the major senses of the word: a state of mind, and a life that goes well for you. More broadly, it is about what it means to live well, viewed through the lens of happiness. I have aimed it at a pretty diverse range of readers. On the one hand I hope it will appeal to ordinary people, young and old, thinking about their priorities. But I have also tried to add something to the scholarly literature and not simply review existing work.

Being a Very Short book, it doesn't cover everything. Not every striking finding from the science of happiness is discussed. Most regrettably, this book does not say very much about non-Western thinking on happiness, nor does it delve into religious thought. This partly reflects my own limitations. But in good part it reflects the growing influence of secular Western ideas in the pursuit of

Happiness: an extremely short introduction

If you really wish to move things along and only want to know what happiness is and how to get it, you could get away with reading just these four chapters: 1, 2, 5, and 8.

happiness. So while I have tried to keep the discussion relevant to readers in most parts of the world, some important intellectual traditions will not be represented.

The social dimensions of happiness also get little attention, beyond the importance of relationships for the personal pursuit of happiness. Yet happiness is not simply pursued at the individual level. How happy we are depends very strongly on the people around us and the kind of society we inhabit. And some of the most pressing questions about our pursuit of happiness concern the way we, collectively, have chosen to seek fulfilment and how it affects our fellow human beings. Not to mention the natural world on which we depend. My children, for whom this book is partly written, do not face an entirely promising future in that regard. For their sake, if not our own, we need to rethink our pursuit of happiness: the dominant approach to seeking happiness in many countries today is, it seems to me, inefficient, destructive, and often self-defeating. But those questions will have to await another book.

I have not tried to be impartial in this book, but rather to develop a more or less coherent picture of happiness and its proper pursuit. Impartial is not terribly interesting, and I have done it elsewhere for those seeking it. But I have tried to show enough of the attractions of competing views to allow the reader to come to her own conclusions.

So let's see, to begin with, what happiness might be.

Chapter 2
What is happiness?

Journal notes, August 8

Sundown on the Pond. A gull is laughing from a perch on a post in the Pond. Now a skimmer glides by, plowing a tiny furrow through the shallows. No permanent mark. Nothing is permanent out here. Sand and water...no mark endures save of notion, of idea...Here the veil between us and the truth of existence is very thin and, to my mind, can be pierced. These past few weeks, I have settled into mindless existence, with few thoughts and no dreams. My being is effortless, untroubled by pain, unstirred by joy. This being is meditative, with no need of mantras or quiet rooms.

Ron Haybron, *Island*

Thriving

A click. Rzzzzzzzz! Line spools off the reel at breakneck speed. A lusty bellow, 'dol*pheen*!' Seconds later, another downrigger pops, and more line starts paying out. Two dolphinfish hooked, and where there are two, there are probably more. (These are tuna-like fish, not the beloved mammal.) Eyes gleaming, Big Joe notes the location of the sargassum patch and leaves the helm to take one of the rods, while his friend Mac takes the other. This is commercial fishing, not sport, so the tackle is heavy and no time is wasted playing the fish. Soon a pair of twenty-pounders are aboard and the boat is circling back for more. Gorgeous fish while alive, a riot of gold, green, and blue, dolphin quickly lose their colour when caught. Occasionally Joe feels a twinge of regret at killing these lovely creatures. But not today. Today he is fully in the moment, locked in on his prey, and whoops with delight as they haul in another pair.

More ballyhoo on the downriggers, more dolphin on the line. 'Gaw-*damn*! Reel's gettin' hotter 'n a [something unprintable].' All told they bring in a couple of dozen, enough for a good profit. Satisfied with the day's catch, Joe puts his twenty-three-foot Sea Ox on a heading for home. A spare, utilitarian boat with twin Mercury outboards and an open cockpit design, the Sea Ox is not for the faint of heart. Not, at least, if you plan to fish forty miles offshore, well into the Gulf Stream, with only a compass and your eyes for navigation. Getting home means hitting a target, an inlet, perhaps a mile across, after hours of meandering through a six-mile-an-hour cross-current. If you do find the inlet, you must thread the boat through some of the most treacherous waters on the seaboard, using throttle and wheel to avoid getting broadsided by a wave or pitch-poling the boat—nose-diving into a trough, flipping end over end. In which case your remains could well become a fine meal for the crabs.

Yet Big Joe Fletcher is in his element. On the long ride home, he is silent, unreflecting, attention fully engaged with the sea, the sky, the boat. Were you to ask him what he feels, he would tell you 'nothing'. He is absorbed in the moment. Passing through the inlet brings a bit of tension, but this quickly fades once they reach the comparatively sheltered waters of the sound. Back at the dock the men share a couple of cans of beer while cleaning the fish, exchanging jokes and friendly gibes with other boaters and passers-by. Joe gives some of the steaks to Mac, keeps some for himself, while the remainder will end up as 'mahi mahi' on the plates of lucky tourists in local restaurants. ('Dolphin', the local name, doesn't go over so well with some diners.)

In the evening, Big Joe and his wife Pam expect to stroll back down to the docks to join the sunset crowd. But some friends drop by and they pass the evening on their front porch, laughter punctuating a chorus of crickets, frogs, and cicadas. An hour later, a couple more wanderers join the fun. Out come a couple of guitars, and the small band of ruffians adds its own music to the nighttime choir.

Things have not always been easy for Joe. He's had his share of romantic troubles and financial difficulties. But at this stage of his life, things are good. The fishing is solid, and between that and the odd carpentry job, the bills get paid. He doesn't need much cash—the house he built himself, and just about any maintenance work on that, the boat, or his truck he can do himself. Many other things can be had by trading with his neighbours.

Joe himself is a big man, in just about every way. A tall, red-bearded man carrying a few more pounds than strictly necessary, and possessed of a booming voice, he carries his bulk with confidence and ease. He does not anger easily, nor is he prone to fret; problems are a part of life, and there's no point worrying. He is big in spirit too: sharp-witted, quick to laugh, exuberant and vital, not given to guile or indirection, he is fully his own man. All the more so since leaving his job at a mainland boatyard. Spending his days at the beck and call of another man never sat well with him, made him feel unnaturally small. Better to be free than a wage slave, even if it means doing without a few things. Big Joe Fletcher is, and feels, free.

You probably won't need much convincing that Big Joe is a happy man. But on what basis would you make this judgement? The description doesn't include Joe's opinion on the matter, and you could well imagine that he doesn't really have one.

In Joe's case, as in real life, we judge how happy someone is not by opinion polling but by observing the person: Do they have a spring in their step? Do they seem tense, tightly wound? Comfortable in their skin? Do they just seem 'off'? Do they laugh easily? Get angry at little things? Burst into tears over minor frustrations?

What we are doing, I think, is trying to assess the person's general *emotional condition*. The term 'emotional' can mislead, since it suggests a narrow focus on feelings like joy or sadness, fear or anger. But being tense isn't really an emotion at all. And what your posture or stride reveals about your 'emotional condition' is something other than an emotion. It's something deeper than that.

We sometimes try to get around the limits of emotion words by speaking of the psyche or soul. Think 'she's in good spirits', or Bob Marley's plea for a lover to 'satisfy my soul'. But I think these sorts of cases involve broadly emotional matters nonetheless, so I will stick with 'emotional condition'.

If this suggestion is right, then much of our everyday thinking about happiness identifies it with a person's emotional condition. Roughly: *to be happy is to have a favourable emotional condition*. Let's call this sort of view an *emotional state theory* of happiness.

So we have a definition of happiness. Is it a good one? Well, we probably can't point to any single definition and say that's *the* correct one. But I would suggest that it's a pretty useful way to think about happiness. It makes sense of the weight people place on happiness, as when a parent says he wants his children to grow up to be 'happy and healthy'. While I will sketch some reasons for preferring this view to the main alternatives, I will not delve deeply into the debate here. Suffice it to say that, while many people find an emotional state account of happiness attractive, I am not describing a consensus view here. The alternatives remain popular as well.

The three faces of happiness

Let's explore this view of happiness in further detail. What exactly does happiness involve? When people think about happiness in emotional terms, they tend to picture a specific emotion: feeling happy. So powerful is this association that happiness frequently gets reduced to nothing more than cheery feelings or 'smiley-face' feelings. This is a radically impoverished understanding of happiness: there's much more to *being* happy than just *feeling* happy.

Think about those periods in your life when you were happiest. Not so much that day when you were elated over a special event, like the birth of a child. Rather, those times of relatively sustained happiness. Not everyone experiences such periods, but if you have, I suspect they looked something like our picture of Big Joe Fletcher, or the photograph of my father and me in Figure 2: good stretches of time wholly absorbed in something you love doing, feeling fully yourself and in your element. Energized, alive, and yet also, deeply settled and at peace—no doubts, no fretting, no hesitation. And yes, feelings of joy here and there, perhaps a good dose of laughter. But those feelings are not the most important part of the story.

2. **The author and his father, sailing**

We can usefully break happiness down into three broad dimensions. Arguably, each dimension corresponds to a different function emotional states play in our lives. But in this book I will skip the argument and simply present the view.

We can think of happiness as a kind of emotional evaluation of your life. Some parts of this evaluation are more fundamental than others. At the most basic level will be responses concerning your safety and security: letting your defences down, making yourself fully at home in your life, as opposed to taking up a defensive stance. I will call this a state of *attunement* with your life. Next come responses relating to your *engagement* with your situation: is it worth investing much effort in your activities, or would it be wiser to withdraw or disengage from them? Finally, some emotional states serve as *endorsements*, signifying that your life is positively good. People often make the mistake of thinking all emotional states are like that.

All three aspects of happiness are important, and different ideals of living can emphasize different parts of the picture. Americans, for instance, put more weight on endorsement or engagement states like joy and exuberance. Whereas Asian cultures tend to focus more on the attunement dimension.

Endorsement: feeling happy and other classic emotions

Let's begin with the most familiar aspect of happiness, the *endorsement* dimension. The most obvious examples here are feelings of joy and sadness. It makes sense for these states to be so closely associated with happiness: they tend to accompany gains and losses, successes and failures.

But it is easy to overstate their significance. While the occasions that call for feeling happy can be important, they may be the exception rather than the rule, even in the best of lives. And such feelings tend not to last very long: you enjoy your good fortune for a bit and then get on with the business of living. If we focus too much on these sorts of feelings, we can easily get the impression that happiness is fixed over the long haul: a simple matter of fleeting emotions that quickly dissipate, ultimately leaving us back at our temperamental 'set point' level of cheerfulness (see Chapter 5).

Yet we should not discount the endorsement side of happiness. In general, it is far better to be cheerful than dour. Life is impoverished without regular doses of laughter. And the generic label, 'feeling happy', conceals a surprising diversity of feelings. Joy, for instance, should not be confused with high-fiving elation. Consider the quiet joy a parent feels when looking in on his sleeping child. By contrast, the jubilation of a sports fan whose team has just scored a goal may be less pleasant, and less fulfilling, even if the feeling is more intense.

Engagement: vitality and flow

The second dimension of happiness concerns your *engagement* with your life: not bored, listless, and withdrawn, but energetic, interested, and engaged. You can affirm your life, not just by giving it a 'thumbs up', but by enthusiastically taking up what it has to offer. This can happen even when things are not going particularly well, for instance when struggling to accomplish a difficult goal.

There are two forms of engagement. The first of these centres on states of energy or *vitality*: what we might call the exuberance–depression axis. A passionate and demanding orchestra conductor, for instance, might be exuberant, even happy, without being obviously cheerful or joyful. I do not know whether the Cleveland's George Szell was like this, but he was evidently quite passionate in living, embodying a kind of exuberance (Figure 3). The mere fact that he was a harsh taskmaster need not disqualify him from happiness. A lot depends on whether his temper often left him deeply unsettled, or simply passed through, leaving little imprint on his inner state.

The exuberant form of happiness is typified in ideals of passionate living, notably in Nietzsche, Goethe, and countless other

3. Cleveland Orchestra Conductor George Szell

romantics and artists. But one need not pursue the passionate life to the Nietzschean extreme. Many people, like Big Joe, lead lives of great vitality without great suffering.

The second form of engagement appears in Aristotle's work, and more recently in the notion of *flow* developed by psychologist Mihaly Csikszentmihalyi. Flow is the state you assume when fully engaged in an activity, typically a challenging activity performed well. Athletes and musicians describe it as being 'in the zone'. In states of flow, you lose all sense of self-awareness, of the passage of time, and are not aware of feeling anything at all. Yet it is a highly pleasant state, and clearly a state in which you are happy. It is roughly the opposite of boredom.

The importance of engagement is particularly clear in cases of depression, where lethargy and listlessness signals a broad psychic disengagement from one's life. This sort of withdrawal is always awful, and sometimes disordered. But it can sometimes be functional, facilitating major life changes by pulling us out of our existing routines and signalling that our present way of living may not be worth continuing.

Attunement: peace of mind, confidence, expansiveness

To understand the third dimension of happiness, consider its most familiar aspect, tranquillity. Tranquillity tends to get the back of the hand these days. People crave entertainment and excitement, and peace of mind can sound a lot like boredom. 'Just give me a Xanax to take the edge off, thank you, and I'll be on my way.'

But I would suggest that tranquillity, or something like it, is the cornerstone of happiness. Perhaps it is possible to be happy without it, but the going will be tough. To see why, we need to get clearer on what tranquillity is. We might think of it as 'settledness': not merely peace of mind or lack of internal discord but a kind of inner surety or confidence, stability and balance. Being imperturbable. The ancient Greeks called it *ataraxia*, Buddhists *sukkha*, and it was perhaps the most sought-after state of mind in ancient religious and ethical thought.

Consider how the happy person looks. While endorsement's characteristic appearance is the smile, and engagement's the jaunty gait, tranquillity presents itself in the relaxed, easy posture. It is clearly a highly pleasant state, and not simply the absence of disturbance or other feeling. Nor does it rule out states of high energy or exuberance, as Big Joe illustrates.

Let's expand on this. Think about the biological condition that states like tranquillity represent. When an organism is in familiar and safe circumstances, where it has mastery of its environment, it can let down its defences and confidently engage in whatever pursuits it wishes. It is this condition, in a person, we are concerned with. The Stoics might have said that the individual in that situation finds her life *oikeion*—familiar—to her. She is utterly at home in her life. In her element.

Similarly, think of the state you assume when relaxing with family, or with an old and dear friend. You feel completely at home with that person. 'Tranquillity' seems too narrow a term for the condition of psychically being at home in one's life.

I will call it a state of *attunement*. In this state a person relaxes and blossoms, living as seems natural to her, without inhibition. The opposite of attunement, disattunement, is not merely anxiety, but more like *alienation*: your circumstances are in some sense alien to you—unfamiliar, imposing, threatening. Defences go up: anxiety, stress, insecurity. Attunement appears to have three basic aspects:

1. Inner calm ('tranquillity')
2. Confidence
3. Expansiveness of mood or spirit. Feeling 'carefree', or being 'uncompressed'.

'Confidence' refers to an emotional condition, not your opinion of yourself. Think about what we might call 'somatic confidence'—feeling wholly at home in your body. Picture, at the negative pole, Nixonian awkwardness. The former president seemed to personify a Cartesian dualism of body and mind gone badly askew. You could have stood *behind* Nixon while he thrust his appendages skyward to signal 'victory' and known immediately that you were not observing an entirely happy man. At the positive end of the spectrum, we might imagine the athletic grace of a ballet dancer.

Contrary to popular stereotypes, attunement arguably forms the core of happiness. Anxiety, stress, insecurity, and related states are not just unpleasant in themselves. They rob us of much of our capacity for the other dimensions of happiness. You might get some measure of cheerfulness while suffering from these forms of disattunement. But exuberance, flow, and joy will be hard to come by. Intuitively, a troubled, anxious, tense, or stressed out person does not seem to be happy, however cheerful she might be. She isn't really at home in her life.

It is easy to overlook the importance of attunement for human well-being, because it does not command our attention like the others do. Take the condition of being *stressed*. Stress is said to be pervasive in the present culture, yet seems not to be taken very seriously. Worries about it are often dismissed as the petty complaints of the rich. Such attitudes are unsurprising since stress usually doesn't monopolize our attention the way, say, back pain can. It can seem more a nuisance than a great problem.

The appearance is misleading, for the main drawback with stress is not the suffering it involves but its corrosive impact on the person. (In one rather more literal way than you might imagine: stress can leave a lasting mark on your genes, increasing your risk of future disease. There is good evidence that your baby can *inherit* those changes, and later on acquire further genetic changes, not to mention changes in brain development, from living with your stress.)

As well, stress compresses and flattens the spirit, smothering your capacity for pleasure. Stressed individuals get less out of life, and indeed there may be less *to* life for them. For their attention is narrowed, and they cannot as easily enjoy, or even notice, what life offers them. The joys of living, the manifold small pleasures that leaven our days are substantially foreclosed when we are stressed. What remains is usually quite bearable, but a lot less worth having.

On a winter morning not long ago, one of the world's leading concert violinists, Joshua Bell, pulled out his Stradivarius and gave commuters in a Washington, DC, subway station a 43-minute virtuoso performance. 1,097 people passed by, many being the sort that routinely pays $100 for a ticket to see him play in a concert hall. Fears of a mob scene proved unwarranted: almost everyone completely ignored the musician, and only seven stopped to listen for even a moment.

A Brazilian shoe shiner who normally dislikes street musicians remarked, 'If something like this happened in Brazil, everyone would stand around to see. Not here.' She continued, 'People walk up the escalator, they look straight ahead. Mind your own business, eyes forward. Everyone is stressed. Do you know what I mean?' The one commuter who recognized Bell exclaimed to a *Washington Post* reporter, whose article was fittingly entitled 'Pearls Before Breakfast':

> It was the most astonishing thing I've ever seen in Washington. Joshua Bell was standing there playing at rush hour, and people were not stopping, and not even looking, and some were flipping quarters at him! Quarters! I wouldn't do that to anybody. I was thinking, Omigosh, what kind of a city do I live in that this could happen?

Mostly affluent in material terms, these busy, disattuned commuters were in some ways quite poor: in this case time poverty. This in turn yields lives impoverished of beauty and wonder. This is not a minor disadvantage. Recall the quote from the Pirahãs that started this book: when asked why a missionary would be visiting them, beauty is the first thing they mention.

The hidden face of happiness

Our sketch of happiness is not yet complete. So far we've considered the felt or experienced side of happiness. But there's more to it than that. Take the fictional case of Robert:

> Robert leads a very active life, and most of the time he is in a good mood: cheerful, smiling, and genuinely feeling good. He also believes that his life is going well and sincerely reports being satisfied with his life. Yet at the end of the day, when he is alone and no longer occupied with things to do, he often feels deeply depressed, sometimes breaking down in tears before falling asleep. He has been like this for several months.

Robert's overall balance of pleasant over unpleasant feelings—his 'hedonic balance'—seems decidedly positive. But is he happy?

Almost no one I've asked thinks so. Of 39 students given the case, only one deemed him happy, and the most common response was 'very unhappy'. About half the students were asked to explain their answers to the question, and only one suggested that his experience was actually unpleasant on the whole. The most common explanation, by a narrow margin, was this: 'deep down, Robert's emotional condition is bad'.

This is interesting. Apparently, many people think you can be unhappy, in emotional terms, even though you usually feel pretty good! What's going on here? According to a long tradition of psychological thought, a large portion of psychological well-being is *unconscious*. On this view, much of what ails us lies buried beneath the surface of consciousness. While we tend to associate such ideas with Freud and his followers, you need not buy into Freudian theory to accept the importance of unconscious states for human well-being. Indeed, virtually everyone nowadays takes the idea for granted, fuelling countless films and novels whose characters' seeming happiness is belied by smouldering distress, just waiting for the right trigger to bring it out. In the film *American Beauty*, for example, the chipper realtor Carolyn Burnham maintains a sunny demeanour that no one in her family mistakes for happiness: beneath the smiles lies a foundation of festering torment, and it is only a matter of time before she snaps (Figure 4).

In Robert's case, his workaday good cheer masks a deeper discord, which he manages to keep at bay with busyness. His emotional condition, though positive on the surface, is decidedly *un*favourable. He is unhappy.

It seems that happiness includes, not just experienced emotions and moods, but the *nonconscious* aspects of our emotional conditions as well. What, exactly, does that involve? Perhaps we need to posit unconscious moods and emotions. I am not sure we know enough about this region of the psyche to say with any confidence. Perhaps all that really matters is that, in such cases,

4. Annette Bening as Carolyn Burnham, *American Beauty*

we are especially *prone* to experience certain moods and emotions. You might have a hair-trigger tendency to become anxious, for instance. Or perhaps you're generally in a good mood, but unusually likely to become irritable or sad. And those propensities alone count as deficits in your happiness.

Let's call this aspect of happiness a person's *mood propensity*: her current propensity to experience certain moods and emotions rather than others. While an individual's temperament tends to be more or less fixed, her mood propensity changes with the circumstances of her life. Cases like Robert suggest that mood propensity is a major aspect of happiness. Ordinarily we don't think much about this side of happiness, because our mood propensities tend to line up with our experienced feelings. But sometimes they do not. A man grieving the recent loss of his beloved wife, for instance, might cope by distracting himself with chores, watching movies, and playing poker. Yet his close friends don't consider him happy, for his calm and good cheer rest on a knife-edge, liable to turn at any moment into anxiety or tears.

27

Happiness as emotional well-being

Let's say, then, that happiness has two parts: your emotions and moods, and your mood propensity. Taken together, these things constitute your emotional condition. So:

> To be happy is for one's emotional condition to be favourable on the whole.

Think of happiness as roughly the opposite of anxiety and depression, or what psychologists often call *emotional well-being*. Since this term already has some currency, I will often refer to happiness as emotional well-being.

An interesting feature of the Robert case is that, if my students' reactions are any guide, it finds virtually no support for one of the most popular theories of happiness, *hedonism*. Hedonists define happiness as a positive balance of pleasant over unpleasant experience. Hedonism is far better known than the emotional state theory, perhaps because people assume that there's no difference between them.

As 'Robert' makes clear, the two theories are different: people seem to grant that Robert's experience is mostly pleasant, but still think him unhappy on emotional grounds. If nonconscious states form the basis for calling Robert unhappy, then hedonism *can't* be the theory people are relying on. Nonconscious states aren't experiences, by definition. So they can't very well be pleasant or unpleasant experiences.

In fact, the differences between the two theories are pretty deep. According to hedonism, to be happy is just for the flow of your experience to be pleasant enough. Happiness is just a sequence of experiences. According to the emotional state view, to be happy is for your psychological *condition* to be a certain way. To assess happiness is to try to figure out a person's basic emotional orientation or demeanour: is she reacting favourably, in emotional terms, to her life? To be happy is essentially to be favourably disposed, in emotional terms, toward your life.

A colleague and leading Buddhist thinker on happiness, Matthieu Ricard, describes a very similar view in these words: 'By "happiness" I mean here a deep sense of flourishing that arises from an exceptionally healthy mind. This is not a mere pleasurable feeling, a fleeting emotion, or a mood, but an optimal state of being.' This state of being, moreover, 'defines the quality of every moment of our lives'. Ricard himself, pictured in Figure 5, is a pretty good example.

5. **Buddhist monk Matthieu Ricard and friends**

Widely reputed to be an exceptionally happy person, he certainly seems that way to me.

You can accept the basic idea of an emotional state theory of happiness without agreeing with my suggestions about the three dimensions of happiness, or the nonconscious side of happiness. If you think about our emotional conditions differently, you may prefer a different version of the emotional state view. Some readers may prefer yet another account altogether, such as the life satisfaction theory. We will take up that theory next.

Chapter 3
Life satisfaction

> 'How's your wife?'
> 'Compared to what?'
>
> Henny Youngman

Two happy men?

One summer night in 1958, Moreese 'Pop' Bickham raised a
shotgun and fired at two sheriff's deputies. Soon, both were dead.
This being segregation-era Louisiana, and Bickham being black,
the act did not bode well for his future. He was promptly
sentenced to death and imprisoned in the notorious Angola State
Penitentiary, the only surprise being that he wasn't immediately
lynched. The facts of the case remain disputed, but Bickham
maintains, plausibly, that he acted in self-defence, firing only after
having been shot himself. The deputies were allegedly Klansmen
out to murder him following a minor argument outside a bar.

Thirty-seven years later, a 78-year-old Bickham was released from
Angola following revelations of an unjust conviction, aided by good
behaviour in prison. He continues to express remorse for killing
the deputies. But on his release, Bickham was asked how he felt
about spending nearly half his life in a Louisiana penitentiary,
including 14 years on death row. 'I don't have one minute's regret,'
he replied. 'It was a glorious experience.'

There were, alas, no happiness researchers in the vicinity. But Bickham comes very close to calling himself satisfied, indeed very satisfied, with his life. It takes very little imagination to suppose that, had he been asked if he was satisfied with his life as a whole, he would have replied in the affirmative. As Bickham 'firmly' averred to a reporter, 'the freest person in the world is the one that's satisfied with what they have'. As many people facing hardship do, he made the best of a tough situation and counted his blessings: 'To live through all this and come out with as much health as I got and the mind that I got, I'm so glad and happy and praising the Lord for it.' There is nothing at all unreasonable about this. In fact it seems something to admire. One of the men who laboured to win Bickham's freedom, radio journalist David Isay, called him 'the most inspirational man I've met'.

Let's suppose Bickham was satisfied with his life, even through much of his ordeal in prison. Should we say that he was *happy* during those years? According to one popular theory of happiness, the *life satisfaction* theory, the answer is yes. There are two things to notice, however.

First, this kind of 'happiness' does not tell us whether Bickham led an emotionally fulfilling life in prison—whether he was in good spirits, at peace, enjoying himself, energized or otherwise in a positive emotional state. Perhaps he was, but that is a different matter from whether he was satisfied with things: life satisfaction is fundamentally a judgement about your life, and you can judge your life favourably no matter how you feel.

At any rate, it is doubtful whether Bickham's life in prison was really pleasant or emotionally fulfilling: we're talking about what is, by reputation, one of the most brutal facilities in the civilized world. Asked if he was like the 'Ice Man' who spent 5,000 years entombed in a glacier, Bickham replied, 'I wasn't on ice, but I was in a can; and they opened the can and I crawled out.' While locked up,

Bickham frequently turned to scriptures for solace; his favourite Bible verse was Psalm 31: 'I am forgotten as a dead man out of mind: I am like a broken vessel.' Now a free man, he prefers Psalm 30: 'Weeping may endure for a night, but joy cometh in the morning.'

I do not think we are compelled to believe that Bickham led a joyous existence in Angola State Penitentiary. And it might seem strange to deem *happy* the 'weeping' prisoner, however satisfied with his life he might be.

The second thing to notice is that, even if satisfied, Bickham may not have thought his life was going *well* for him. In fact it seems rather plausible that he did not: he plainly thinks it vastly better to be free than 'in a can', and is hardly unaware of how much of his life passed him by.

> When I first went in, I had only one daughter, now she's got eight children and they got 24 children. All that happened since I been locked up. It makes a man think, 'How in the world (did) all this happen, and I've got to be away from it?'

He might very well have thought, 'Well, my life is going *terribly*, but at least I've got my health and my wits. What God has given me is more than I have any right to expect, so I'm satisfied.'

To be satisfied does not mean you think your life is going well for you, by your own standards or any other.

If we say, then, that Bickham was happy in prison because he was satisfied with his life, that leaves entirely open whether he had a pleasant or otherwise decent emotional life, or whether he saw his life going well by his standards. It tells us only that he figured it was going well *enough*, however badly that might be.

This might seem a rather curious theory of happiness. You would not be out of line to wonder why anyone should care very much about being happy, if that's all it amounts to. If this is happiness, who needs it?

Perhaps Pop Bickham is a little hard to evaluate, since he seems to have such an upbeat personality. Having little more than the happy ending to go on, it may not be easy to picture the long dark nights of sorrow.

If so, then I offer for your consideration Ludwig Wittgenstein, the famously tormented philosopher who, dying young from an illness, reportedly said to 'tell them I had a wonderful life'. Sometimes called the most important philosopher of the 20th century, it seems not unreasonable for Wittgenstein to have said this about his life, which was certainly interesting and filled with accomplishment. But *happy*? Look at his picture (Figure 6). The man looks like he was born seeing a ghost. This is the sort of 'wonderful life' that one should not wish on the meanest kid in town, and I sorely hope that none of my children experience Wittgenstein's particular brand of wonderfulness. The fellow oozed misery, to the point that his brother Paul, a concert pianist, once protested that 'I cannot play when you are in the house, as I feel your skepticism seeping towards me from under the door!' If you're still not convinced, I recommend a visit to the house he designed for his sister in Vienna, architecture being another of his pursuits. The soulless domicile reeks of gloom, and not even Wittgenstein liked it despite having laboured intensely over it for two years. Nor did his sister, who somewhat surprisingly was not among the three Wittgenstein siblings to commit suicide—the philosopher himself nearly becoming a fourth. And yet, Wittgenstein was evidently satisfied with his life.

As many researchers define happiness, these men were happy. So too are the 6–7 per cent of respondents in one study who claimed

6. Ludwig Wittgenstein

to be 'completely satisfied' with their lives, though they also believed themselves to be *'usually unhappy or depressed'*. Could this be happiness as we know it?

The life satisfaction theory of happiness

While hedonistic and emotional state theories roughly take happiness to be a matter of *feelings*, life satisfaction is normally thought of as mainly being a matter of *judgements*. There are lots of ways to interpret the notion of life satisfaction, but here I will focus on the most common and compelling version of the view. To be satisfied with your life is to regard it as going well enough by

35

your standards: taking all things together, you see your life as having enough of the things you care about. So life satisfaction is a global evaluation of your life. There is something very appealing about this view of happiness: it takes you to be the authority about your life, and ties your happiness to your view of what matters for you.

People often call life satisfaction a 'hedonic' good—a good of pleasure—lumping measures of life satisfaction in with measures of feelings. This is a mistake. The whole reason for focusing on life satisfaction instead of feelings is precisely that it is *not* just a question of pleasure. Most people care about lots of things besides their own pleasure, and life satisfaction seems to reflect that fact. A high-achieving artist or scientist might be satisfied with her life even if it isn't terribly pleasant: she's getting what she cares about. Life satisfaction seems distinctively important because it tracks people's values. At least, it seems like it should.

How important is life satisfaction?

And yet it doesn't, at least not in the way you might expect. People can quite reasonably be satisfied despite feeling bad, and *despite thinking their lives are going badly for them.* As we saw in the case of Bickham, that you are satisfied with your life tells us surprisingly little about how well your life is going in relation to what you care about.

Why should life satisfaction be so loosely related to our own sense of how our lives are going? There are two basic reasons for it. First, life satisfaction involves making a *global judgement* about your life. But lives are complicated mixtures of good and bad. You might be glad about having an interesting job, impressive hang-gliding skills, a loving family, and a functioning laptop, but not so glad about that back problem, the creepy friends your kids hang out with, that lie you told your husband, or your parents being deceased. And so on, ad-for-all-intents-and-purposes-infinitum. How does it all add up? Who knows?

Life is not a gymnastics routine. If you try to boil your life down to a single number, the result is bound to be pretty arbitrary. (Even gymnastic scores tend to involve a fair dose of whimsy.) Given how you see things, you might just as easily label your life a 4 or a 7. The fact that you happen to report a seven, in this case, doesn't mean your life is going any better than if you'd offered up a four. It's a coin toss.

Second, life satisfaction involves a special kind of global judgement about your life: a judgement about whether your life is going, not just well, but *well enough* for you. Is your life satisfactory? If you think about it, that's kind of a strange question. Satisfactory compared to what? 'Compared to your goals or aspirations', one might say. But *how much* must you succeed in your goals to reach the 'satisfactory' point? Will getting 12 per cent of what you want suffice, or do you require 74 per cent? Or 100? Is this even an important question?

We often have some idea how to answer such questions about consumer products. If you order a steak well done and it comes out rare, for instance, you have pretty clear expectations and an obvious remedy: it isn't satisfactory, so you send it back. If your life has some nasty bits, though, what should you conclude? Life is not a consumer product. You can't very well send it back for an upgrade, or shop somewhere else next time. Anyway, the price of admission is free: you're just born, and there you are. So it's hard to know where to set the bar for a 'good enough' life. You might choose to be satisfied with a 2, or require an 8 to be satisfied. The fact that you're satisfied with your life may simply mean that you've dropped the bar so low it would take a catastrophe to get you to be dissatisfied. It sure beats being dead.

And so, having made an arbitrary decision about how to add up all the goods and bads in your life, you must make another arbitrary decision about where to set the bar for 'good enough'. A coin toss on top of a coin toss. It may not seem that way, because we often settle into a standard way of making these judgements. For instance, unless things are really bad or really good, you might just say 'fine', or 'pretty satisfied'. Which may be why answers to life satisfaction questions so often converge on the 75 per cent mark of whatever scale you choose: don't want to complain, but not perfect. 'Fine.'

Because we lack any compelling reason to arrive at a particular judgement of life satisfaction, we are free to base our judgements partly on things that have no bearing on how well our lives are going. You may decide to focus more on the positives because you care about virtues like gratitude or fortitude. Perhaps you'd feel like an ingrate being dissatisfied with your life. Or maybe you focus on the positives when things are bad to cheer yourself up. But if you register satisfaction with your life because you don't want to be a complainer, that doesn't tell us much about how well you see yourself doing.

So the fact that people in hard circumstances report being satisfied with their lives does not tell us that they're doing well. Slum dwellers in Calcutta tend to say they're satisfied with their lives, but that leaves entirely open whether they think their lives are going well for them. As the title of the paper reporting this finding suggests, perhaps they're just making the best of (what they see as) a *bad* situation. Similarly, large long-term studies of Germans and Britons found most people claiming to be satisfied with their lives *throughout the experience of their spouses dying, or becoming unemployed*. It is unclear whether they really thought their lives were going well for them during these hardships. When asked to explain why they are satisfied with their lives, Egyptian study participants did not always reply, 'because my life is great'. Instead, they said things like:

A person adapts himself to his conditions, I accept my destiny.
One day is good and the other one is bad, whoever accepts the least
lives.
God wants this. Whoever is satisfied says thank God and whoever is
tired says thank God. We cannot do anything.

Which are just so many ways of saying, 'life is pretty much a kick
in the groin, but what can you do?' This is probably not the sort of
happiness you had in mind for your kids.

Worse, satisfaction can respond perversely, or not at all, to
important changes in our lives. Dialysis patients in one study
reported life satisfaction no lower than healthy individuals, yet
also stated that they would give up *half their remaining life-years*
to regain normal kidney function. In other words, their life
satisfaction reports failed to register a colossal dissatisfaction,
probably because they coped with the illness by comparing
themselves with other patients.

In a study of colostomy patients, those with permanent
colostomies actually reported *higher* life satisfaction than patients
with temporary colostomies. Why? A permanent colostomy means
needing to wear a bag to hold your waste for the rest of your life.
Is that really better than a temporary one? Most likely, the ones
with no hope of improvement simply lowered the bar for a 'good
enough' life. Doing worse from their point of view, but more
satisfied.

You might have thought it important that people be happy.
But if by that we just mean life satisfaction, then a world of
admirably positive-thinking prison inmates, languishing
in *what they see as* unfulfilling, unpleasant, and stunted lives, should
do the job nicely. This is not a very inspiring notion of happiness.

It can be hard to get one's mind around the idea that life
satisfaction is not terribly important. When we picture the

satisfied person, we tend to imagine certain stereotypes: Aunt Greta reflecting on a highly successful life, say. And since most people seem to report being dissatisfied only when things are truly dismal, that's our image of the dissatisfied person: Uncle Bob ruing his ailing health, failed aspirations, and crumbling relationships.

But what's significant in these cases is not so much the *judgement* of satisfaction or dissatisfaction: it's the success or failure of their *lives*. Aunt Greta's life would still be successful if, duly noting her fulfilling career of high achievement, she concluded that it should be still better: thriving, but dissatisfied. And Uncle Bob's life would still be a catastrophe if he lowered the bar and decided that, well, it could have been worse: miserable, but satisfied. It seems to make only a modest difference whether they are satisfied. But shouldn't it make a huge difference whether they are *happy*?

There is little question that when people speak of happiness, they sometimes have life satisfaction in mind. So it is not quite a mistake to call the merely satisfied 'happy'. But it is probably misleading, and not very helpful.

How life satisfaction does matter

None of this shows that life satisfaction studies can't provide useful information. Even if it isn't very important whether people are satisfied with their lives, knowing whether one group is *more* satisfied than another can tell us about *relative* levels of well-being. Exceptions duly noted, people reporting higher life satisfaction tend on average to be doing better in realizing their values. They report greater satisfaction with specific things in their lives, and generally tend to be doing better on other measures as well. This could be true even if *everyone* set the bar so low that they would be satisfied with just about any life. Still, the problems we've been discussing raise significant worries about life satisfaction measures. Since it seems important to know how people see their lives going, researchers may want to develop better ways to get this information.

There is an interesting corollary to the idea that the vast majority of people could reasonably be satisfied with their lives. As we will see in the last chapter, it suggests that most people actually have good lives. Not in the sense of being well-off or flourishing, but in the broader sense of having choiceworthy lives—lives they could justifiably endorse. Lives one could, when delivering their eulogies, reasonably deem 'good'.

Bickham and Wittgenstein probably weren't making a mistake in affirming their lives. On the contrary, they seem actually to have *had* good lives: lives worth affirming, warts and all. The mistake is ours: supposing that life satisfaction tells us whether people are doing well or thriving. Apparently, it does not.

What is happiness? Summing up

Summing up the message of the last two chapters: emotional state theories of happiness make intuitive sense and explain the importance we attach to being happy. The rest of the book will assume such a view. Hedonistic theories also vindicate the seeming importance of happiness, but don't seem to fit the ordinary notion of happiness very well. Life satisfaction theories have some intuitive plausibility, but can't seem to make sense of the value we place on happiness. 'I just want my kids to be happy' might be a little exaggerated. But it sounds a lot more compelling than 'I just want my kids to be satisfied'. If you want them to be satisfied, suggest they think of Tiny Tim and count their blessings.

Chapter 4
Measuring happiness

> Happiness in intelligent people is the rarest thing I know.
> Ernest Hemingway

The challenge

Can happiness be measured? The short answer is yes...sort of. To get a sense of the challenges, imagine a pair of communities, Eudonia and Maldonia. Here is one facet of life in these places:

- On a typical day in Eudonia, a typical resident is liable to be at ease, untroubled, slow to anger, cheerful, quick to laugh, fulfilled, in an expansive and self-assured mood, curious and attentive, alert and in good spirits, and fully at home in her body, with a relaxed, confident posture.

- In Maldonia, the average person tends to be stressed, anxious, tense, irritable, worried, weary, blue, distracted and self-absorbed, uneasy, awkward and insecure, spiritually deflated, pinched, and compressed.

I suspect many readers will agree that Eudonians are generally happy, while Maldonians are unhappy. Not only that, but this is a very important fact about them. When deciding how to live, the greater happiness attending the Eudonian way of life is surely a

major point in its favour. In fact it takes some work to imagine
how Maldonia could, realistically, be a better place to live.

Good measures of happiness should tell us that Eudonia is
happier than Maldonia. They should also convey something of the
size of the difference: Eudonia should rate much higher on our
happiness scales than Maldonia. Can our measures of happiness
accomplish this?

You might think something as complex and elusive as happiness
would be impossible to measure. And you'd have a point: precise
measures of happiness are out of the question. We'll never be able
to assign an exact number to how happy a person is.

For most purposes, though, the science of happiness can get by
with rough measures that tell us, on average, which groups of
people tend to be happier. And which sorts of things tend to make
people more or less happy. For these questions, we don't need
exact measures, and many errors tend to wash out when
comparing large groups of people. The reason is that you'll get the
same errors in each group, so any differences between the groups
probably aren't due to error. For instance, maybe people
understate their happiness slightly on rainy days, because the
weather gets them thinking more negatively. But the fact that
people with jobs report higher happiness than the unemployed is
probably not an effect of the weather. It would be quite a
coincidence if unemployed people just got asked on rainy days,
while people with jobs only did the questionnaire on sunny days.
More likely, unemployed people do worse on the happiness
measures because they *are* less happy.

Think of it this way: most people seem to agree that depression
and anxiety questionnaires are useful for figuring out how
depressed or anxious people are. People who score really poorly on
a depression survey probably aren't in a great mood. But notice
that these just *are* happiness questionnaires. The only difference is

that they focus on certain kinds of unhappiness. Measuring happiness is no more mysterious or fraught than measuring depression and anxiety. And it should be no more controversial.

So serviceable measures of happiness are easier to come by than you might think. In fact almost all the measures currently in use tend to track the sorts of things you'd expect them to: smiling, health, longevity, stress hormones, friends' reports, and so forth.

What to look for in measures of happiness

Many of these measures still leave a lot to be desired. Probably the least useful are surveys that simply ask people to say how 'happy' they are. Since people interpret the word 'happy' differently, different respondents will effectively be answering different questions. Some people may think the researchers want to know if they're satisfied with things, while others take it to be a question about their emotional well-being. (Consider how differently Wittgenstein might have answered these questions.) Researchers need to make up their minds which meaning of happiness they're interested in, and use measures that clearly track *that*.

Other measures ask people about life satisfaction, which at least has a fairly clear meaning. But we've seen that this is quite different from happiness in the emotional sense that we're talking about here.

If we *had* to limit ourselves to a single question, it might take the form of asking people to rate their emotional conditions on a scale from, say, 'depressed and stressed' to 'joyful and relaxed'. Still, it is not easy to sum up your entire emotional life in a single number. Better measures would make detailed inquiries into people's emotional conditions, asking about each of the three dimensions of happiness. For instance: do you feel angry right now? Stressed or worried? Do you feel 'slowed down', lacking energy? Or: did you laugh or smile a lot of the time yesterday? Did you get caught up in an interesting activity? Are you able to enjoy things these days? Have you been quick to get angry lately? And so on. Through such questions we can get a rough sense of a person's emotional profile and make broad comparisons.

Future measures will likely go beyond these sorts of self-reports, looking as well at stress hormones, brain imaging, and voice and facial expression analysis, among other things. But for now, most of our evidence about happiness relies on self-reports.

When reading about scientific studies of happiness, it is wise to bear three caveats in mind:

1. *What is the study measuring?* Ideally, a self-report measure of happiness should have multiple questions assessing all major aspects of emotional well-being—for example, attunement, engagement, and endorsement.

2. *Do the groups being compared tend to answer happiness questions differently?* For instance, Italians might have a 'don't get me started' culture that puts less of a positive spin on things than Americans, whose default is 'can't complain'. So an Italian might report lower happiness than an American even if they are equally happy.

3. *If the study claims that some group of people is 'happy', what's the evidence?* Most studies like this are talking about life satisfaction, not happiness in the emotional sense. And if they are talking about emotional well-being, there's a problem: we don't know *how* happy people must be to qualify as 'happy', versus 'not-happy'. Let's see why.

How happy is happy?

Suppose we find that people experience more positive feelings than negative. Can we conclude that they are happy? The standard answer is 'yes'. Yet it's not clear anyone has ever seriously defended the idea; it has just been assumed. This is an extremely shaky assumption. Remember the case of Robert, discussed earlier: he clearly has more positive than negative emotion, yet he is just as plainly unhappy. Offhand, a life in which one feels bad nearly as much as one feels good doesn't sound very good at all. Suppose you have nine bad meals for every ten good ones, get nine pokes in the eye for every ten orgasms, etc. That sounds awful. In fact many philosophers have offered a very similar threshold for a life that's barely worth living: a life where the pleasure just outweighs the pain. You might have thought there was a considerable distance between happiness and a life that's barely worth living. Which in turn is just a shade better than being dead. Be happy or die?

English philosopher John Stuart Mill (1806–73) wrote that happiness involves 'an existence made up of few and transitory pains, [and] many and various pleasures'. That sounds more like it, though we should want to focus on emotional states rather than pleasure. Can we make it a little more precise? Some research points to a threshold of around three positive emotions to every negative emotion. Above this threshold, people may tend to do well in a variety of ways. Whereas things generally go worse when the ratio of positive to negative emotion drops below 3:1. I suspect the truth will prove to be a little more complicated than that. But this much seems plausible: *happiness probably requires an overwhelming predominance of positive over negative emotional states*. In which case most researchers are working with the wrong cutoff for happiness, overstating how many people are happy.

This is not an academic point: if someone is happy, people tend to figure that he is probably doing well. If he's unhappy, that he's doing badly. So when studies pronounce that most of the population is happy, the natural conclusion is that most people are doing well. So why not move on to more pressing problems?

Suppose, for example, that happiness does requires a 3:1 ratio of positive to negative affect. In that case, some of the evidence that supposedly shows most people are happy may actually support the *opposite* conclusion. A study of Germans, for example, found that people's emotions were negative about 34 per cent of the time. This was believed to support the idea that most people are happy. Yet it might actually be evidence that most people are *not* happy. That's a pretty different conclusion!

Are people as happy as they say they are?

However, the studies tend not just to say that most people are happy. They tend, rather, to say that the *overwhelming majority* of people are happy. In an oft-cited 1976 study (Figure 7) of Americans, for instance, 93 per cent of people claimed to be happy, with only *3 per cent unhappy*, and 0 per cent choosing the most negative of the seven options. A 2007 Gallup poll found 92 per cent of Americans reporting happiness, with only 6 per cent 'not too happy' (the closest thing to a negative option). Remarkably, 98 per cent of respondents with household incomes over $75,000 reported happiness, while only 2 per cent proffered 'not too happy'. In one of the largest worldwide surveys of happiness, the World Values Survey, 94 per cent of Americans reported being happy in 1995.

This is a proportion commonly known as 'everyone'. As in, 'As everyone knows, we've landed men on the moon'. Strictly speaking, 6 per cent of Americans don't believe that. But you can get 6 per cent of the population to say just about anything. And yet it's quite a chore to get even that fraction of the public to say they're unhappy.

Faces Scale : "Which Face Comes Closest to Expressing How You Feel About Your Life as a Whole ?"

20%   46%   27%   4%   2%   1%   0%

7. The 1976 smiley-face chart

Since even in the best conceivable society we should expect some people not to be happy at any given time—death in the family, incurable disease, foolishness, etc.—the 94 per cent figure indicates we are in the vicinity of a theoretical limit. In terms of per cent happy, we may be doing about as well as a society possibly can. Except for Iceland, where 97 per cent claim to be happy. In fact a number of countries match or exceed the United States, and Venezuela and the Philippines trail close behind, at 93 per cent.

The majority of people may indeed be happy. People may well be happier than we tend to think. No doubt intellectuals do have a tendency to overstate the quantity of misery in the world, as Hemingway probably does in the quote above.

But these numbers are preposterous. Even the faintest acquaintance with living, breathing human beings makes such figures wildly implausible. I'm not saying the results are meaningless; higher numbers probably do tend to signal happier people. It's just that they're plainly inflated: in no important sense of 'happiness' could that many people be happy, either now or at any time in recent memory.

For starters, about 1 per cent of Americans are incarcerated. Three per cent are under the supervision of the criminal justice system. But maybe they're happy anyway. Let's consider some more direct evidence.

Depression and anxiety: in studies of the United States, the percentage of purportedly 'non-happy' people, which includes both the unhappy and those who are merely OK, roughly equals the rate of major depression. Not just the blues, but the crippling affliction that tends to make its sufferers want to die. In fact about 12 per cent of the population appears to have either major depression or a generalized anxiety disorder at any given time. In 2006, 11 per cent of adults under 44 took antidepressants. On any given day, around 16–20 per cent of Americans report having felt sad 'a lot of the day yesterday'.

One reason may be loneliness. In one large study, Americans reported having only two confidants on average—individuals with whom they can discuss important matters. Over half have no friends in whom they can confide, and a quarter of Americans have no confidants at all. A leading expert on loneliness, neuroscientist John Cacioppo, estimates that 'at any given time, roughly twenty per cent of individuals—that would be sixty million people in the U.S. alone—feel sufficiently isolated for it to be a major source of unhappiness in their lives'.

How about stress? In 2007, one-third of Americans reported extreme levels of stress, rating their stress an 8–10 on a 10-point scale. Three-quarters reported physical symptoms from stress in the last month, with 36 per cent of people so strung out that their stress made them want to cry. The same number said they skipped a meal due to stress. Not surprisingly, 10–15 per cent of Americans suffer from chronic insomnia.

The data on children raise further questions about the hypothesis of near-universal happiness. Consider these recent findings, mostly concerning affluent children:

- In a study of 15,000 American college students, more than half said they'd contemplated killing themselves at some point in their lives. Eight per cent had actually attempted suicide.

- A study of 10th grade girls in an affluent American suburb concluded that 22 per cent had clinically significant symptoms of depression and anxiety.

- In a study of 633 American 9th and 10th graders in the South and Midwest, 46 per cent engaged in self-injury or self-mutilation over the past year. The most common forms were cutting/carving skin, burning themselves, and hitting or biting themselves. (At the national level, estimates tend toward 10–20 per cent.) Another study found such behaviours in 17 per cent of Princeton and Cornell students.

- In Taiwan, where 89 per cent of adults report being happy, 16 per cent of 10–12-year-old children make themselves vomit to lose weight.

These figures do not scream 'overwhelmingly happy society'. Or, for that matter, healthy or perhaps even sane. It is certainly not an inevitability that a society's young people want to kill themselves. Now the numbers do not rule out the possibility that a majority of people in the United States, or Taiwan, are happy. Some results may not hold at the national level, and any single study may have defects. But it is basically impossible that 94 per cent of Americans are happy, at least in the sense of emotional well-being. Clearly, the self-reports are a little inflated.

People might tend to overstate their happiness for two reasons. First, 'positivity biases' infect the way we think about ourselves: we tend to have overly rosy views of ourselves and our futures, a phenomenon known as positive illusions. While cultures vary in the extent to which they exhibit positive illusions, it is plausible that, when asked how happy they are, most people tend to skew their responses toward the positive side of things.

Second, we lack clear standards of what it means to be happy. The notion is pretty vague in most people's minds. Which means you have lots of licence to call yourself happy without actually lying. Unless you're a complete wreck, you can probably get away with judging yourself happy without being baldly dishonest. And if you can honestly get away with calling yourself happy, why not? If you're not at an Alcoholics Anonymous meeting, why would you say you're unhappy if you don't have to? As a general rule, people don't say they're stupid or ugly unless compelled by some pretty indisputable facts to do so. Luckily, those concepts are vague enough that such facts are hard to come by. Similarly, probably few people call themselves unhappy unless things are so grim that there's no truthful way around it.

Again, this doesn't mean the measures aren't telling us a lot about *relative* levels of happiness: who is happier, and what things tend to go with greater happiness. They can probably tell us that Eudonia is a lot happier than Maldonia. But they can't yet tell us very much about how many people are actually *happy*. Aside from obvious cases, like depression and bulimic ten-year-olds, we just don't know.

Chapter 5
The sources of happiness

Breathe in. Breathe out. Breathe in. Breathe out. Forget this and
attaining Enlightenment will be the least of your problems.

A Jewish joke

Some questions

Listing the sources of happiness is a surprisingly tricky business.
One problem is figuring out how to divide things up. Do we focus
on relationships? Friends and family? Community? Love?
Different researchers often use different concepts, and there's no
'right' set of concepts to use.

A second difficulty: what matters for happiness depends a lot on the
kind of society you live in. In parts of Papua New Guinea, happiness
might depend on how many cassowaries you own. In most other
places, I would venture, the preferred number of these disagreeable
birds is approximately zero. And while some of the tribesmen who
trade in cassowaries may have little use for money, you will find it
hard to get by in Beverly Hills without a *lot* of it. The importance of
money for happiness hangs substantially on where you live.

So there's no simple, general answer to the question, how
important is money for happiness? Just as there are no simple,

general answers to the questions of how important cassowaries, fishing nets, telephones, or cars are for happiness. It depends. This is a screamingly obvious point, but one rarely noted. One of the choices societies have to make is not just how to promote the sources of happiness, but what things they are going to *make* important for happiness.

Still, we know that certain things tend to make a big difference in happiness just about everywhere. Take a randomly selected infant and imagine that she could be placed in any society, at any time. What sorts of things will have the most impact on her happiness over the course of her life? Which items would be most important to get right? Even if there's no single 'best' way to list these items, there's a lot of agreement about the general shape a list should take.

Genes and set points

The influence of genes on happiness has gotten a lot of press. Perhaps you've heard that at least 50 per cent of happiness is genetic, the product of your innate 'set point' level of happiness. I won't say much about such claims in this book. First, there's nothing we can do about it, or nothing we should. Second, no one seriously maintains any longer that genes have so much influence that there's nothing very much anyone can do to promote happiness. This is why researchers bother to compile lists of the sources of happiness. Even if people do have happiness set points, it is obvious that plenty of things can affect how happy we are, for a long time. A bad job, for instance.

There is a kernel of truth in the set point idea: human beings are remarkably adaptable and resilient. Over time, we tend to adapt to most changes in our lives, ending up roughly as happy as we were before. Accordingly, this chapter focuses on the most important things we *don't* adapt to: the things that make a lasting difference in how happy we are.

Our genes hardly determine our destinies. Scientists try to discover the influence of genes on happiness by studying how 'heritable' happiness is: roughly, how much of the variation we see in people's happiness is due to differences in their genes. People make lots of mistakes when talking about studies of heritability. To move things along I won't explain the intricacies, but will simply offer an example. In one paper on the heritability of happiness, the authors famously suggested that trying to become happier may be 'as futile as trying to be taller'. We're trapped on a hedonic treadmill, with no hope of progress. This is plainly false and has since been rejected by at least one of the authors. But while it is indeed hard to make yourself taller, the pursuit of greater height is not futile at all. Improved living conditions have raised the stature of men in the Netherlands by 8 inches in the last 150 years. They went, that is, from being short, at 5-foot-4, to being tall, at over 6 feet today. Yet height is certainly more heritable than happiness.

If we can do for happiness what modern societies have done to make people taller, that will be an enormous achievement.

The sources of happiness: SOARS

What, then, are the chief sources of happiness? I will focus on five items that researchers generally agree on. These are, in no particular order (except to provide a usable acronym):

1. Security
2. Outlook
3. Autonomy
4. Relationships
5. Skilled and meaningful activity

The constituents of this list are well-established in the scientific literature. In essence, I have extended the list of universal human needs proposed by psychologists Richard Ryan and Edward Deci. They posit three basic needs for autonomy, competence, and relatedness. To this list I have added two other items: outlook and security. While Ryan and Deci's 'eudaimonic' approach to well-being is somewhat controversial, the importance of these items for happiness is generally a matter of consensus, with the possible exception of autonomy.

Security

The plainest necessity for happiness is that you don't feel under threat: you feel secure in the possession of what matters. This can seem pretty obvious on the face of it. Nobody expects to be happy when the bill collector comes knocking.

But the role of security in happiness is more complicated than it seems. There are different kinds of security, and the sorts that matter for happiness are not always what we might expect. Physical risk, for instance, need not cause anxiety even if we are aware of it. Rock climbing is not the world's safest pastime, yet climbers often describe clinging to a sheer cliff face, just one tiny mistake from death, as a *calming* activity. The Pirahãs lead far more perilous lives than most of us, yet seem about as untroubled as anyone you're likely to meet (Figure 8). Come to think of it, the physically safest people seem often to be the most anxious, worried, or stressed. This may not be coincidental: activities involving some physical risk tend to focus the mind, quieting the din of intrusive thoughts and worries that so often occupy and distract us.

In short, the security that matters for happiness is *perceived* or felt security. At least three sorts of security seem particularly important for happiness. Thus far we have focused on perceptions of *material* security. Again, this can be somewhat independent of actual material security. In fact wealth can breed material insecurity, inflaming the appetites, raising expectations, and habituating us to high living. This makes us needier, more vulnerable to disappointment, frustration, and anxiety. The point is fairly obvious, and nothing new. Epicurus, the ancient Greek hedonist, had this advice on how to lead a pleasant life: avoid

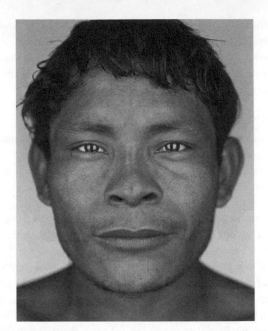

8. Xopi, a Pirahã man

luxuries and live simply. Luxurious living turns you into a needy person whose happiness depends on things easily lost. The Stoics offered similar advice, as do Buddhists, whose philosophy centres on eliminating the cravings that make us vulnerable to suffering. Remarking on his study of very wealthy Americans, researcher Robert Kenny observes:

> Sometimes I think that the only people in this country who worry more about money than the poor are the very wealthy. They worry about losing it, they worry about how it's invested, they worry about the effect it's going to have. And as the zeroes increase, the dilemmas get bigger.

Affluence is a double-edged sword: it can buffer us from many ills and sate some of our wants. Yet it also tends to increase those wants and creates new vulnerabilities. It may indeed leave some people feeling *less* secure. One feature of the modern consumer economy aims precisely at making that happen: the point of much advertising is to sow dissatisfaction, making people want what they didn't want before.

A second major form of security is *social*: feeling secure in one's relationships and standing in the community. Given how profoundly social human beings are—see 'Relationships', below—this form of security is particularly important.

Third is what we might call *project* security: feeling secure in the prospects for success in one's major projects. By projects I mean commitments or goals with which you identify: they form part of your identity or sense of self. A career or vocation can be a project, as can being a good parent, or finding a cure for some disease. You can succeed or fail in your projects, and the fear of failing can be a potent source of unhappiness. Because you identify with your projects, your self-esteem depends on how you do in them. When you fail, it can feel as though *you* are a failure. This is a pretty terrible feeling, as is the anxiety that comes with merely suspecting that you might fail.

One of life's choices, for those of us privileged enough to have such choices, is how far to stake our fortunes on the pursuit of risky projects. Starting a business, for instance. Such projects are often highly rewarding, meaningful, and worthwhile. But the pursuit of high achievement also tends to bring greater project insecurity: worry, anxiety, and frustration. There's a tradeoff to be made, and no single 'best' way to resolve it.

The least obvious form of security is *time* security: feeling that you have sufficient time to do what you need to do. The lack of it, for the most part, is what we call being 'stressed'. People who lack time security to the extent of being chronically stressed probably tend not to be happy. This is both because being stressed diminishes happiness in itself, and because it tends to ripple through our psyches, leaving us irritable, anxious, oblivious to the good things around us, and generally stripping the texture and pleasure from our lives. While a little stress can be a good thing, 'stressed' and 'happy' do not readily combine.

But again, there are interesting nuances. Some people take great satisfaction from fast-paced lifestyles, having barely enough time to get everything done. A chef might be like this, and her daily routine may be something of a dance. On good days everything gets done, and done well, but only *just*. This can be invigorating, but it is not—save on bad days—stressful. Needless to say, such a lifestyle is hard to pull off without a lot of stressful days. Again, it is a question of tradeoffs.

Security is good for happiness, but more is not always better. Too much security can make us complacent, lazy, soft, and weak, stunting personal development. A coddled, risk-free childhood can be a recipe for an unhappy adult, unable or unwilling to persevere through hard times and unequipped to handle the uncertainties, dangers, frustrations, and setbacks of everyday life. Result: 'boomerang' and 'failure to launch' kids who require parental care well into adulthood, gratuitous divorces between overgrown children, vocational dilettantism…

I trust these worries are familiar to many readers today. Here in the United States, many children are kept largely indoors under close adult supervision, with few opportunities for spontaneous or self-managed play with other children. The 'nightmare' scenario that seems chiefly to motivate such extreme measures is a stranger kidnapping the child, whose parents will never see her alive again. Since you can't be too careful, some parents purchase dental 'toothprinting' services to ease the future identification of their (now rather alarmed) child's mangled or charred remains. A US Department of Justice assessment of this seemingly ubiquitous horror found that it occurred 51 times over the course of a year, in a nation of 300 million. That's 51 times too many, but also roughly the same number killed by bees, wasps, and hornets. A risk of approximately zero.

One does not often hear parents say, 'I would never let my child run around the neighbourhood; bees might get him.' For comparison, horses claim an estimated 219 lives a year in the United States. Another 17,000 lives are lost from falling down, and 36,000 expire from the flu. One way to promote happiness is to take a rational approach to risk.

Outlook

'Happiness is a choice. It's all about your attitude.' This is probably the most oft-heard advice oft-heard about the pursuit of happiness, at least in my neck of the woods. Similar claims pepper the self-help literature. There is a good point being made here. But taken literally, such claims are nonsense. A typical depressed person can no more will himself into happiness than he can sprout wings and fly. Admonishing him that he can perfectly well be happy if only he so chooses is foolish and cruel. It is rather like telling a cancer victim it must be her fault she's dying, because people with a good attitude stay healthy. Happiness is not a choice.

Yet the hyperbole does not arise out of thin air: our outlook does play a large role in determining how happy we are. And we do have substantial control over our attitudes, even if not as much as the merchants of cheap sunshine would have us suppose. True, if your temperamental starting point is dour Eeyore, then the perkiness of Tigger is not going to be a realistic aspiration for you. And if you live in Manhattan, you may have a hard time managing a laid-back New Orleans demeanour. But within broad limits we can do much to alter our outlook in ways that leave us happier.

The Stoics believed that well-being is entirely within the individual's control, depending wholly on your character. Socrates held this view as well, arguing that the many cannot hurt us, even by torturing and killing us, so long as we retain our virtue. What matters is not what happens to you, but how you respond to it. And the true sage, according to the Stoics, would remain unperturbed no matter what happens. Socrates himself is actually a pretty good example here. Similarly, Buddhists believe we have it in our power to achieve happiness by rooting out craving, the source of suffering.

But happiness, in these views, is not something you simply choose, like a pair of shoes. Rather, it is a *skill* you must cultivate through years of effort. None of these thinkers holds the crazy view that anyone can just pick up a book and bootstrap herself into happiness. There are enough unhappy Buddhists in the world to make clear how nontrivial the task is.

But with the right effort, we can develop an extraordinary degree of control over our internal states. Matthieu Ricard, pictured in Chapter 2, refers to the discipline of meditation as 'mind training'. Reporters dubbed him, with characteristic exaggeration, 'the world's happiest man' after a study found remarkably 'happy' patterns of brain activity. In a number of studies, Ricard has displayed exceptional powers of self-awareness and control. He describes and recounts emotional experiences with uncanny detail and accuracy when checked against his physical responses. In one study researchers subjected him to a loud noise like a gunshot while meditating. He showed little of the normal startle response. This is not normally thought to be the sort of thing a person can control. As Ricard described the experience, 'I was not actively trying to control the startle, but the detonation seemed weaker, as if I were hearing it from a distance.' A study of other meditators found them capable of raising the temperature in their fingers and toes by more than 17 degrees Fahrenheit. Such individuals can tolerate remarkably cold temperatures without evident discomfort—as in, sleeping on a Himalayan ledge at zero degrees Fahrenheit wearing nothing but a shawl.

One doesn't have to be a Buddhist to learn something from mind training techniques. As I write, I am on a plane headed home from a draining trip. Seated behind me are two children, 6–8 years old, and their mother. The kids are not exactly quiet, and the lameness of their mother's pleas for them to pipe down is not terribly relaxing either. I am incensed. And then, taking a lesson from Ricard, I turn my attention from the scene behind me to my reaction to it. Why am I getting mad? Is my anger helping anything? Is it reasonable to expect perfect children, or perfect parenting? I don't need to answer these questions; simply attending to them causes the emotion to dissipate. I relax and my attention returns to my work.

Then the man in front of me slams his seat into full recline, crushing my kneecaps. Repeat cycle, as needed.

What sort of outlook tends to promote happiness? There's no obvious candidate for 'best' outlook; each has its pros and cons, and works for different people. As well, 'outlook' covers a lot of ground: for example, how we tend to perceive, interpret, explain, evaluate, and respond to things, and what we value.

Two approaches tend to dominate discussions of outlook and happiness: *positivity* and *acceptance*. Positivity is pretty self-explanatory: focusing on the positives, savouring life's little pleasures, being optimistic and grateful, counting one's blessings, etc. Seeing the humour in things, letting oneself be silly or ridiculous.

Acceptance roughly means not getting bent out of shape when things don't go your way: accepting things as they are, and not demanding that they fit your agenda. Keeping expectations modest. This can sound defeatist to some, but that's not the idea: you can have this outlook and still have high hopes, and still work hard to make things better. (The Dalai Lama is not exactly a slacker, nor is Ricard.) But you'll more easily shrug it off and move on when things aren't the way you'd like them to be. You won't be as needy as the person with outsized expectations. And you might be better poised to appreciate the good things in life, instead of seeing them through the lens of your appetites.

A third kind of outlook with important benefits for happiness is *caring for others*. Research indicates that people who care more about others tend to be happier. This is partly because being happy tends to make people more sociable and concerned about others, but there is also a strong effect in the other direction. Helping others is well-known to be a potent happiness booster. Psychologist Michael Argyle reports that among leisure activities, only dancing generated higher 'levels of joy' than volunteer and charity work. Other studies find that people get more happiness from spending money on others than using it themselves. To caring I would want to add moral concern more generally, including a strong sense of moral integrity: being honest and keeping promises, for instance. There does not seem to be much scientific research on the question, but philosophers have long pressed the idea.

9. Man giving his shoes to a homeless girl in Rio de Janeiro

The ancient hedonist Epicurus, for instance, claimed pleasure is our sole end in life, yet firmly counselled being just and otherwise virtuous: it is essential, he thought, for peace of mind.

The final kind of outlook has to do with the motives that drive your work and other activities. Having materialistic values, for instance, tends not to make us happier. Studies find that people who place a higher value on money, possessions, and status tend to be less happy. Those with less materialistic values tend to be significantly happier. More broadly, people driven primarily by external rewards like wealth or status tend to be less happy than those who see their pursuits as intrinsically worthwhile, doing them for their own sake. Researchers call the latter *intrinsic motivation*, the former extrinsic motivation. In the workplace, workers who see their job merely as a paycheck or a career take up the instrumental attitude toward their work: just a means to getting something else (money, promotion...). And they tend to have much less satisfying work experiences than those who see their work as a 'calling'. (Usually I prefer less grandiose terms like 'vocation' or 'trade'.) The difference isn't in the job itself but in the worker's attitude: janitors and trash collectors can adopt the calling orientation and see their work as intrinsically meaningful and fulfilling.

Notice that you can be rich, or have materialistic desires, without having particularly materialistic *values* or priorities. The question is what you really care about, and poorer people are often more materialistic than the rich. You can perfectly well enjoy shopping and dreaming of expensive purchases without actually caring whether you get those things. As a child, I eagerly awaited the arrival of the Sears and J. C. Penney Christmas catalogues each year. But it never occurred to me to think it mattered very much whether I got their contents, which I usually did not.

Summing up, at least four kinds of outlook seem to be especially productive of happiness:

1. Positivity
2. Acceptance
3. Caring for others
4. Intrinsic motivation

Outlook shapes happiness at the cultural level as well. People in the United States clearly get a happiness bonus from the powerful streak of optimism, cheerfulness, and friendliness that runs through the culture. Latin American countries like Venezuela, Colombia, Panama, Costa Rica, and Mexico appear to boast remarkably high levels of happiness, all the more so given their modest material holdings. They consistently rank at or near the top of international happiness studies. One reason seems to be the relatively strong family and community ties in these nations. But a good deal of the impact seems to be cultural: Latino cultures tend to emphasize the enjoyment of life—celebrating, slowing down, hanging out, and rolling with the punches. Colombians have a saying, when frustration strikes during one's travels, as when the car breaks down: 'Todo es parte del paseo.' It's all part of the ride.

Once, while living in Tucson, my wife and I were wandering a desolate stretch of town at dusk, baby in tow, trying in vain to find a restaurant. We were bickering mildly about how to proceed. A homeless Latino man approached. He didn't want a handout. He wanted to administer a scolding. 'What's wrong with you? You have a beautiful family. Look at all you have. You should be happy!' Coming from a homeless man, this was a little humbling. But he was right.

Autonomy

> I concealed my departure because it was embarrassing for a Maasai warrior to run away from home in search of employment....The Maasai would say he went looking for servitude.
>
> Tepilit Ole Saitoti

If you have lived with a small child, then you know how profound the human urge is to do things for oneself, and make one's own decisions. 'I want to open the door myself!' The drive for autonomy runs deep in human nature, and a sense of control over one's life is an important source of happiness. People who feel able to make their own decisions, without being under another's thumb, tend to be significantly happier. And perhaps even healthier as a result: nursing home residents have been found to be happier, healthier, and live significantly longer if given even a modicum of autonomy. For instance, being in charge of plants in their room rather than having them cared for by the staff.

Freedom, in short, is a major source of happiness. But some kinds of freedom are more important than others, and more freedom isn't always better. The kind of freedom we are talking about here, *autonomy*, has to do with self-determination. Autonomy, in this sense, is about whether the individual is in charge of her affairs. It is freedom from coercion, meddling, and being subject to another's will.

Running a small business, for instance, is risky, hard work, yet small business owners often report high levels of happiness: not having a boss ordering you around is highly appealing. In fact this is a tremendous shortcoming of the wage economy, easily lost on us because of its ubiquity: to be an employee is to be subject to another's whims. It used to be called 'wage slavery', and some people still regard it that way.

Autonomy should not be confused with another kind of freedom, *option freedom*. This is the freedom of having a range of options to choose from. Is this important for happiness? The evidence is mixed, though people with greater option freedom do seem, on average, to be happier. The impact of money, discussed later, is the clearest case: money essentially benefits us by giving us more options.

Now clearly people do not need lots of options to be happy: hunter-gatherers have few options in life, but at least some of them like the ones they have and manage to be quite happy. Still, option freedom can allow an exit from bad situations and make it easier to obtain things that make us happier. Many people, myself included, pursue rewarding occupations that would have been closed to them in a traditional community or totalitarian state, where one has little choice but to work in a certain factory or tend the family farm, whether one likes it or not.

As well, simply having options can yield a liberating and pleasant sense of possibility. For example, the demand for cars in China and many other places is fierce, probably due in no small part to the simple feeling of freedom they can give us. The vision of rolling down an open highway into the sunset is, for many people, profoundly attractive.

On the other hand, option freedom comes with a price. Obviously, your odds of making a mistake go up. But choosing among more options is also harder work, and can be anxiety-provoking. Sometimes people respond by avoiding the choice altogether (decision avoidance). Bad outcomes become less a matter of blind luck, to be shrugged off, and more an occasion for regret and self-reproach. And options can weaken commitment and contentedness, making our relationships, possessions, and projects seem more contingent and dispensable. One reason for the rise in divorce rates, for instance, is almost certainly rising discontent owing to greater perceptions of viable alternatives to one's spouse. (Think about it this way: if you were stuck on a desert island with someone, you'd probably figure out how to get along.) Barry Schwartz, the leading researcher on the costs of choice, entitled a review of the literature on these effects 'The Tyranny of Freedom', and a recent book *The Paradox of Choice*.

Autonomy is often derided as a narrowly Western, individualistic ideal unsuited to many cultures. Such complaints seem unlikely to impress the legions of Egyptians, Tunisians, Libyans, Syrians, Yemenis, and others who have risked life and limb in the Arab Spring uprisings. Ideals of self-determination have spread across the globe for good reason: human beings do not generally like being pushed around.

The critics correctly note that Western-style individualism has little purchase in many parts of the world. In more communal or 'collectivist' cultures like those in Asia, Africa, and Latin America, people identify themselves more strongly with their families and communities, place more stock in fulfilling social roles and expectations, and have less concern for privacy and self-gratification. This strongly affects what they *want* to do, and it does mean that people give greater weight to the attitudes and interests of others in their decisions. In fact your life is not entirely your own, but is intertwined with the lives of others. In some 'big picture' matters, as in whom to marry, you might have little choice. Still, you may have control over a large part of your life. For example, being in charge of your daily routines may matter more for happiness than the big-ticket items simply because they are always before you, always foreground. Even in areas where you lack complete control, you can be autonomous in the sense that you act for reasons you endorse; you don't feel coerced by your parents, say.

At any rate not all communal cultures are coercive. In fact some have strong taboos against anyone telling another person what to do. Parts of Southeast Asia are said to be like this, for instance, as are many hunter-gatherer societies. In such places people may be strongly autonomous, yet in a non-individualistic way: living as they freely choose, but giving more weight to communal concerns than individualists do. In the most recent World Values Survey, people in 57 countries were asked to rate 'how much freedom of choice and control' they feel they have over the way their lives turn out. In general, answers to questions like this are among the better predictors of happiness and satisfaction. As expected, Americans did pretty well on this metric. But the strongest sense of personal freedom and control was actually reported by the 'collectivist', and not especially rich, Mexicans and Colombians.

Relationships

'All you need is love', the Beatles told us, and they weren't too far off the mark. To say that relationships matter for human happiness is like saying water matters for fish. Of all the things that matter for happiness, relationships are probably the one thing we most need to get right: family, friends, and community.

Relationships most plainly benefit us by allowing us the pleasures of each other's company. Talking and doing things together are potent sources of happiness. Studies that track how people feel during different activities find that people—introverts included—experience more positive emotions when in the company of others. Socializing consistently ranks as one of the most pleasant activities.

Naturally, close relationships are important. In a study of highly happy individuals, every one of the subjects turned out to have very strong relationships. Psychologists Ed Diener and Robert Biswas-Diener sum it up nicely: 'the close relationships that produce the most happiness are those characterized by mutual understanding, caring, and validation of the other person as worthwhile'. Inside and outside of close relationships, being treated with respect is important, as is having the esteem of those whose judgment matters to us.

These are pretty mundane points, yet easily forgotten or misunderstood. My father was mainly raised by his grandmother, and one of his most vivid recollections of her parenting style was simply that she paid attention: if her grandson came to her with something to say, 'Mom' would drop what she was doing, lower her glasses, and give him her full attention. That simple gesture demonstrated his worth to her, and boosted his own sense of self-worth, more than any heap of toys could.

One of the better signs of friendship and community is trust. To have a confidant, for example, is to have someone you trust with your most private and important thoughts and concerns. If the people in a neighbourhood trust each other enough to feel comfortable poking gentle fun at a bad haircut, then they probably form a community in the fullest sense of the word. Unsurprisingly, measures of trust correlate pretty well with measured happiness. Trust is so important because it provides a sense of security: we feel accepted, loved, and protected, with a network of people willing to sacrifice their interests for us. Having that kind of security is a crucial buffer against adversity, a safety net that is hard to live without. Ideally, we will spend most of our time among people who provide that sense of security.

This can be hard to do in many societies. Employment in bureaucratic organizations like corporations or government agencies can be pretty depersonalized even if in some sense highly 'social': you may spend most of your days in the company of people whose interest in you is primarily self-directed, and who you don't particularly trust. For most of human history, children seem to have spent the vast majority of their time surrounded by people who love them unconditionally. Today, most children in industrialized nations spend the bulk of their weekdays in institutional settings among hired caregivers whose affection, distributed among 10, 20, or more children, is largely contingent.

In the United States, for example, it is not unusual even for 5-year-olds to find themselves ostracized by the community for ordinary behavioural problems, with no refuge outside the immediate family, if they even have that. (I have witnessed this several times in affluent American communities. In each case, the effects on the child ranged from inflammatory to devastating.) Opportunities for playing with other children outside of school are often mediated by parents, who set up the necessary appointments for 'play dates'. The parents, of course, are unlikely to invite this child to their homes. In that event the child has little chance to develop friendships or to learn from a community of peers how to negotiate the social world. He just gets punished and shoved aside. It does not take a peer-reviewed study to figure out what this does for a child's happiness.

A strong community not only provides a sense of security; it makes many things easier and lessens the need for money. Fewer expenses for child care and entertainment, for example. A nice television is less important if you have someone to talk to. If something breaks, a neighbour might help you fix it. In the process you both get a social occasion and the pleasures of giving and receiving, perhaps benefiting more than if you'd had the money to just buy a replacement.

Skilled and meaningful activity

Perhaps the two most important facts about human nature, from the perspective of happiness, are these: we are *social* creatures, and we are *agents*. Lovers, and doers. We've covered the 'social' bit, so now let's turn to the agency part of the equation. In general, people are happiest leading active lives—doing, and not just having or passively consuming. Watching television, for instance, rates as a modestly pleasant activity, but closer to the pleasantness of a nap than of hanging out with friends and family. And it seems to have little impact on happiness.

Activity matters, but not just any kind of activity. Passing one's days performing a mindless, pointless, repetitive task is no one's idea of happiness. The basic structure of happiness-making activity was recognized long ago, by Aristotle. For Aristotle, the most pleasant life is a life of virtuous or excellent activity. He basically means the exercise of our capacities through worthwhile activities done well. Well-being, on his view, is not a state we achieve but, more or less, something we *do*: the activity itself constitutes our flourishing. And to live in this way brings the fullest happiness we can achieve.

The research seems to bear him out on this. The activities most productive of happiness appear roughly to have two features, each implicit in Aristotle's view: they are *skilled* and *meaningful*. The state of flow, for instance, is a peak form of happiness that tends to arise when doing something well, particularly a challenging activity that pushes one's skills to the limit. Playing an instrument or a sport well, for instance. At one point, Aristotle literally defines pleasure as 'unimpeded activity'. Not only are people happier while experiencing flow, but having frequent experiences of this sort appears to boost happiness generally, even when not doing the activity. To the extent that money correlates with happiness, a major reason may be that better-paying jobs are more likely to involve regular experiences of flow, and otherwise give people the opportunity to exercise their capacities.

But the exercise of skill alone may have little impact on happiness if you don't see the activity as worthwhile or meaningful. An attorney expertly arguing a dishonest case for a deplorable client might have flow experiences while doing it, but be left deflated and depressed at the end of it all. Playing video games can provide flow but usually isn't very fulfilling, even if flow normally entails at least some sense of meaning due to the exercise of skill.

Meaning is so important that I devote a large portion of Chapter 7 to it. There I will suggest that the most meaningful activities involve *appreciative engagement*, or connection, with people and things that matter. And emotional fulfilment might arise only through this sort of activity: a fulfilling life probably requires appreciative engagement with people and things that seem to you to matter.

Nature and other sources of happiness

Our list of the causes of happiness could be longer. Other things commonly cited as major causes of happiness include religion, not being unemployed, achieving goals, good government, self-esteem, etc. Most of these items probably contribute to happiness primarily through the five channels in the SOARS model.

Think of a childhood experience—whatever first comes to mind. Does it involve being with other people, or out in nature? I once found myself in a fairly diverse group of about a dozen people who were asked to describe one childhood memory. Except for one individual who recalled a bad event, every single story involved a nature experience. Loved ones also featured in most of them.

Contact with the natural world may be a further item to add to the SOARS model. A fast-growing body of literature indicates that contact with nature has a remarkably powerful impact on human happiness and health. Simply having a view of trees or other natural scenery may help sick people recover faster. Immersion in natural environments is both calming and revitalizing, and significantly improves attention. Indeed it appears to be effective in treating attention deficit disorder. Contact with nature confers a wide range of benefits, and may be a significant human need. (Some of my urbanite friends recoil at such claims, but I suspect one reason cities are so appealing is that they offer a highly stimulating sensory experience—closer to the richness of a natural environment than, say, a featureless suburb.)

I leave nature off the list because we lack the data to confirm that the gains are powerful and distinct enough to warrant inclusion. But for those who have spent much time living close to the land, the profound disconnect between daily life and the natural world in many places today is liable to seem a bit insane. As if we were born in the Louvre, but chose to live in the broom closet.

Money: the cost of happiness

As I noted at the start of this chapter, there is no fixed amount of 'importance' of money for human happiness. Even if money were really important for happiness at all incomes today, it wouldn't follow that we should strive for more money. Maybe we should. Or maybe we should try to change our economic arrangements or personal priorities, in turn changing the role of material wealth in our lives. Maybe we should try to make money less important to us.

The point is not that money is a bad thing. On the contrary. It's that we shouldn't underestimate our options. Findings about the money–happiness relationship don't settle what we should do: we can accept that relationship and pursue happiness accordingly. Or we can *change* that relationship: we can decide, to some extent, how important to make money for happiness. The cost of happiness is not fixed.

Writer James Martin, for example, abandoned a lucrative but gruelling career at GE and took a vow of poverty, becoming a much happier Jesuit priest. In so doing, he radically changed the importance of money in his life. His choice obviously isn't for everyone, but it illustrates the kind of control we have in this matter.

That said, we do have many studies on the relationship between money and happiness in the world as it is today. In a nutshell, the message is this: for the poorer members of a country, money seems to have a fairly strong impact on happiness. But above a certain point, the relationship is quite weak. In the United States, happiness and income show a pretty substantial link until about $75,000 household income, above which the lines for emotional well-being go more or less flat: on average, the impact above that point is roughly zero. (See Figure 10.) In places with a lower cost of living, the point of negligible returns may be lower. A study in Monterrey, Mexico found no increase in self-reported happiness for a family of four above an income of just $4,000 a year. Looking worldwide, the relationship between income and happiness appears generally to be weak. This may be partly because poorer people tend to live in poorer countries, where it takes less income to meet basic needs.

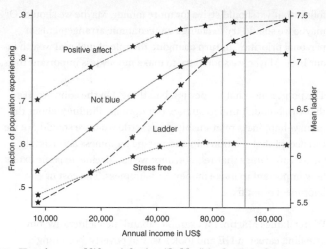

10. Happiness and life satisfaction ('ladder') in the United States

Income and *life satisfaction*, by contrast, seem more strongly related, even for wealthier people. (This result, note, is often put in terms of 'happiness'.) In general, people with more money tend to report higher life satisfaction. To some extent, this probably reflects the role of money in helping people get the things they care about. Money can do things for us even if it doesn't make us happier: get our children a better education, or keep us more secure against unexpected calamities.

But it is possible that life satisfaction measures artificially inflate the money–satisfaction link, for reasons related to the problems raised in Chapter 4. For instance, richer people may tend to be more positive-thinking, reporting higher satisfaction even when not getting more of what they care about. As well, people might tend to focus more on material priorities than other important values like family and friends when answering life satisfaction questions, because their everyday concerns focus more on things like paying the bills than having friends.

A further point is that richer people often enjoy many advantages besides spending power, like greater autonomy, better government, and stronger social support. Denmark, for instance, is a wealthy country that also happens to be one of the world's happiest countries; but it also scores very highly in other areas known to be important for life satisfaction and happiness. Once you control for those other factors, the relation between money and life satisfaction becomes much weaker.

Money is clearly important for most of us. But it seems to be a lot less important than many people would have guessed. Let me close with a brief illustration of one reason the relationship might be so modest. One of the happier places I've known is a remote village of fewer than 1,000 residents that, while not poor, also does not have a lot of money to throw around. Beyond a few small stores, the nearest shopping is a couple of hours away. Mail is not delivered to your home, so you have to go to the post office to pick it up. These are inconveniences, yes, but they also bring great advantages: the post office and general store are social hubs where you'd best have a lot of time to spare, as you might easily pass an hour catching up with some neighbours. The difficulty of buying things means people rely on each other for help getting things done, again building relationships. And when an old friend turned another year older, several hundred people—a large fraction of the village—threw her a surprise birthday party. It may be no coincidence that so many residents seem to reach a very advanced age, sticking around for a *lot* of birthdays.

Conclusion

The findings we've been discussing have a couple of interesting upshots. First, happiness doesn't require a whole lot: human needs are pretty simple and commonsensical, and we might do well not to get too fancy in the pursuit of happiness. Stick to the basics, and you can do pretty well.

Second, the pursuit of happiness can't be just an individual matter. The *context* in which you live is also a large part of the story. Your relationships depend a lot on where and with whom you live, as do your opportunities for meaningful and engaging work, your ability to live as you choose, your sense of security and ability to relax and enjoy life, and even your outlook. Yes, you have a lot of choice over these things. But they also aren't totally up to you. To a great extent they are things we have to pursue together, by building better communities and a better society.

Chapter 6
Beyond happiness: well-being

Tell me now whether a man who has an itch and scratches it and can scratch to his heart's content, scratch his whole life long, can also live happily.

Socrates, in Plato, *Gorgias*

The need for more than happiness: 3 cases

'I just want my kids to be happy.' 'As long as she's happy, that's all that matters.' People often say things like these. Are they right? Is happiness the only thing that matters? We can understand how people might be tempted to speak this way: as a general rule, happy people probably tend to be faring well; unhappy people, badly. How happy we are is central to the quality of our lives. But it probably isn't the only thing that matters, or even the most important. From here on out, we will be looking at how happiness fits into a good life.

We begin with this question: what ultimately benefits a person? What is it to thrive or flourish? In short: *what is the nature of well-being?* The notion of well-being should not be confused with the concept of happiness, or 'emotional' well-being. That is a purely psychological notion, just like the concepts of pleasure, depression, or anxiety. Well-being, by contrast, is ultimately a matter of *value*: what is good for us? What sorts of lives should we wish for our children, for their sake?

There are several reasons to doubt that happiness could be the only thing that ultimately benefits us. Well-being seems to require more than just being happy. To see why, consider three problem cases.

Deception

Imagine yourself living sometime in the future, in a world of amazing technology. Scientists have invented an extremely sophisticated 'experience machine' that can simulate any reality you desire. Do you want to be Paul McCartney? Jane Austen? How about a walk on Mars? No problem: the machine can make you believe you're really doing these things, and really are these people. Indeed, life in the experience machine is indistinguishable to you from life in reality. Once plugged in, you will have no idea it's merely a simulation. By now experience machines have become supremely reliable, and you have the opportunity to connect to one. Not just for an evening, but for the rest of your life. Life from that point on will be as pleasant and satisfying as you wish.

Would you plug in? Most people say they would not. In a new study spanning ten countries around the world, majorities in every nation rejected the idea of plugging into the machine. In most countries the rejection rate was higher than 80 per cent. Indeed, people tend to find the idea appalling, recalling dystopian fantasies like *The Matrix* or *The Truman Show*. Or, more realistically, persons blissfully ignorant of their spouses' or friends' treachery. These are not people we envy.

Apparently, most people care about things other than their states of mind. They seem to want actually to succeed in their goals, really to achieve things, truly to do things, and genuinely to have loving friends and families. They want to be happy, but they want their happiness to be grounded in reality. Better, and better off, to be less happy and lead a real life.

Philosopher Robert Nozick first proposed the experience machine example, which I've tweaked a bit here, in 1974. It has been hugely influential, and is widely taken to show that neither happiness nor any other state of mind can be the sole measure of human well-being.

Impoverishment

Socrates, in Plato's *Gorgias*, has us imagine a decidedly untextured life: someone who is content to do nothing but scratch an itch.

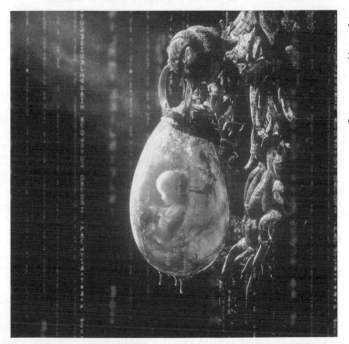

11. A baby starting life in its 'experience machine' pod, *The Matrix*

That's the sum total of his life. Is this an enviable existence? Rawls gives a similar example of a grass-counter, happy to do nothing but count blades of grass all day long. Most people find such lives unappealing, if not downright depressing. There's not much to such flat, featureless, one-dimensional lives. It seems better to lead a life rich with varied activities and experiences. To be able to say you really *lived*.

Similarly, few of us really aspire to be 'couch potatoes', squandering our precious minutes of life on solitary, cheap entertainments, while not actually doing much. Imagine a slob who passes his life alone in a filthy basement doing nothing but watching television and playing video games, living off his inheritance. This is the passive life of rank pleasure-seeking Aristotle dismissed as fit only for 'dumb grazing animals'. Homer's lotus eaters, who laze about all day whacked out on narcotic drugs, raise the same concern. Contemporary films like *Wall-E* and *Idiocracy* depict further variations on the theme. Few parents, I suspect, would wish such lives for their children.

Perhaps scratchers and couch potatoes seem so unappealing because we value personal development, or self-actualization. It seems important to develop and exercise our capacities. Notice how the popular ideal of 'flourishing' suggests the full flowering of one's human powers. The scratcher, the couch potato, and the lotus eater can seem to be squandering their potential, however pleasantly they spend their days. In such cases the individual's life appears to be stunted or *impoverished*.

Deprivation

There is a young woman, 20 years of age, who looks like a baby of about that many months. The woman, Brooke Greenberg, has an extremely rare disorder called Syndrome X, which appears to stop intellectual and physical development beyond the toddler stage. Yet there's no reason to think that she couldn't be pretty happy.

She appears to have a lovely, loving family that cherishes her, enjoys her company, and regards her as a great blessing just as she is. Perhaps, in periods where Ms Greenberg is happy, we should say she is doing well, with a high level of well-being. Still, it is hard to escape the feeling that someone who never reaches maturity is missing out on certain elements of a normal, full life. It seems that there's *something* to be regretted.

We need to be cautious here. I am not saying that a disability makes a person or a life any less valuable. Nor that she can't do well, indeed flourish. Still less that we should feel sorry for her. Those of us with friends and relatives who have disabilities, or who have disabilities themselves, know how irritating and condescending pity can be. In some ways a disability can enrich a person's or a family's life. It often brings out the best in people, making us better and more focused on the things that really matter, than we would otherwise be.

But it is also silly and patronizing to insist that there's no downside *at all* to most disabilities. In cases like Syndrome X and certain other disabilities like blindness, it can seem as though one is *missing out* on something, deprived of one of the elements of a full life. Of course the point does not just apply to disabilities. We can have the same concern for someone who dies young, never experiences the pleasures of sexual intimacy, or, like Pop Bickham, spends whole passages of life in prison, never able to watch his children grow up. Many feel that such a deprivation is an irreplaceable loss. Not least, many such individuals themselves. A priest or monk who takes a vow of celibacy, for instance, may lead a rich and fulfilling life. Perhaps he gains more in other goods than he loses. But he may yet see it as a sacrifice, giving up an important aspect of human life in order to achieve other values. From his own perspective he misses out on something, and no amount of other goods can wholly erase the sacrifice.

So however well-off a person may be on the whole, there still seems to be something to regret, an irreplaceable loss, if she fails to enjoy one of the cherished elements of an ordinary life. It may be important, not just to be happy, but to lead a *full life*, missing out on nothing. (Note that a deprivation does not mean you can't lead a 'full life' at all. Leading a full life, like many things, comes in degrees. Even if priestly celibacy involves a deprivation, many priests still lead full lives.)

Not everyone finds these three cases persuasive. Some people react differently to them, and most theories of well-being, including my own, run afoul of at least one of these cases. Sometimes our intuitive reactions to things are just mistaken. So we must take these cases with a grain of salt. That said, many people find them pretty compelling.

What ultimately benefits a person?

Introducing Aristotle

In Western thinking about human well-being, no figure outside of religion looms larger than the Greek philosopher Aristotle. His views remain popular today. This is a bit surprising, since his outlook on well-being was decidedly un-modern. According to Aristotle, well-being, or *eudaimonia*, can be given a rather striking definition: it is a complete life of virtuous activity. Virtue for Aristotle is not simply moral virtue, as we tend to think of it today, but human excellence generally. It includes not only obvious virtues like justice and bravery, but prosaic talents like being able to tell a good joke, or carrying yourself with dignity. In today's terms, 'excellence' probably works better than 'virtue'. But bear in mind that we are talking about *human* excellence: displaying the excellences characteristic of human beings. His standard of virtue was not subjective, but rooted in universals of human nature. Excellence in collecting bottle caps or selling shady investments would not cut it.

Notice that Aristotle did not simply identify the good life with having a virtuous or excellent character: you could slumber through life, like Sleeping Beauty, with a good character. And who needs that? A good life, rather, consists in excellent *activity*: it is more something you do than a state you try to attain.

To illustrate: poverty doesn't rule out being virtuous, but it can get in the way of exercising human excellence. When your best option is to spend 90-hour weeks doing monotonous sweatshop labour, your opportunities to spread your wings and fully exercise your capacities are few and far between. Poverty is bad, for Aristotle, because it so sharply limits your functioning. In the worst cases, it can leave you unable to live much like a human at all, reducing you to the condition of an animal scrounging merely to survive.

You can, I hope, see the attractions of Aristotelian thinking at this point. What a 'life of virtuous activity' really means is fully exercising your human capacities, actively pursuing a rich, full life. Such a life is deeply fulfilling too: the most pleasant life a person can lead. Many people find this sort of idea highly appealing when they think about it, and contemporary culture is rife with variations on the theme, for instance in exhortations to 'be all you can be'.

The general theme is that what's good for us is to fulfil our natures: *nature-fulfilment*. There are different ways of understanding nature-fulfilment, but Aristotle's is the best-known. The ideal of nature-fulfilment was widespread among ancient Greeks who wrote about *eudaimonia*. Accordingly, we might call such views of well-being 'eudaimonistic' theories. This family of views has become fairly popular among psychologists lately, giving rise to a movement of 'eudaimonic' psychology.

One of the great virtues of Aristotle's approach to well-being is that it seems to give an attractive explanation of our intuitions about all three cases discussed above: deception, impoverishment, and deprivation. In the experience machine, you aren't really doing anything at all. The scratcher is pretty much the opposite of the Aristotelian ideal. And some disabilities deprive individuals of important elements of a full human life.

For all its virtues, Aristotle's theory of well-being remains deeply controversial. Some don't like its objectivism: Aristotle thinks there are objective facts about what's good for you, and they don't depend entirely on what you like or care about. Many reject this idea, holding that well-being must be subjective. A deeper problem, I think, is that Aristotelian accounts apply an *external* standard of well-being to individuals: what's good for you is to lead a characteristically human life. Similarly, what's good for a bull is to lead a characteristically bovine life, doing what bulls do. But why should your well-being depend on facts about what species you belong to? Take Ferdinand the bull, from the children's story (Figure 12). He's a bit of an oddball who doesn't want to fight or do other things normal bulls do. He'd rather smell the flowers. And why not? The whole point of the story is that it doesn't matter what's typical for members of your kind: all that matters is what *you're* like.

12. Ferdinand the bull

(The careful reader may have noticed that the 'Ferdinand' point does not sit easily with the 'Syndrome X' point: how can we say that Syndrome X deprives one of anything unless we apply an external standard, looking at human norms? On this score Aristotle's view better explains the Syndrome X case, while the approach I endorse later does better with the Ferdinand case.)

Another popular objection targets the Aristotelian claim that well-being is a matter of virtuous activity. But is it really? Genghis Khan was a rotten person who butchered millions and impregnated a rather disturbing proportion of our great, great ....great grandmothers. (One in 200 people alive today appear to be directly descended from him.) But why couldn't he have been happy, even flourishing? Given the human aptitude for killing, he might have been an *exemplar* of human thriving.

Virtue is extremely important, as we'll see in the next chapter. But many doubt Aristotle's view that virtue necessarily *benefits* us.

Theories of well-being

Where does this leave us? It will help to get a quick sense of what the options are. Probably the four most influential approaches to well-being are these:

1. Hedonism
2. Desire theories
3. List theories
4. Eudaimonistic ('nature-fulfilment') theories

We've already discussed the best-known eudaimonistic theory, Aristotle's. At the other end of the spectrum, *hedonists* claim that only pleasure is ultimately good for us. Such views ably capture the manifest importance of enjoyment and suffering in human life. But they also have trouble dealing with all three puzzles that started this chapter: deception, impoverishment, and deprivation.

Desire theories assert that what's good for you is getting what you want. This is a very popular view, especially among economists, since it seems to make you the authority about what's good for you. On the plus side, experience machines aren't a problem for desire theories, since you won't *actually* be getting what you want. You'll merely think you are. But desire theories have trouble explaining mistakes. Generally, it seems obvious that people often want things that aren't good for them, like desiring a date with someone who turns out to be a jerk, or wanting to be a lawyer. Nor can they say that there's any deficiency in the seemingly impoverished life of a scratcher, or a slave who embraces his servitude. Likewise in some cases of deprivation, where the person has no desire for the missing goods (as in Syndrome X).

List theories identify well-being with a list of objective goods. For example: knowledge, achievement, friendship, and pleasure. If you are lacking something on the list, then your well-being is compromised, even if you don't want or like it. List theories have the advantage that you can put whatever seems important on the list, making short work of most problem cases. They have the disadvantage that this can seem pretty arbitrary, and not very illuminating about the nature of well-being.

None of these objections is clearly decisive: all these views continue to have smart defenders. They either reject the intuitions we've been discussing, think the alternatives are even worse, or try to modify their account to deal with the intuitions. Desire theorists, for example, often claim that only informed and rational desires count. But the basic worries have not been decisively rebutted, and the modified theories have serious problems of their own.

Eudaimonism for moderns: self-fulfilment

Let's come back to the eudaimonistic approach. Perhaps we can find a theory that shares Aristotle's focus on fulfilling our natures, but isn't so strongly objectivist. In his justly famed essay on the value of individuality in *On Liberty*, British philosopher John Stuart Mill portrayed a more modern, individualized ideal, which we might call *self-fulfilment*: living in accordance with *who* you are—the self. On the ideal of self-fulfilment, well-being is a matter of your individual personality, however eccentric that might be.

What's normal for humans, on this view, is irrelevant for what's good for you, just as what's normal for bulls doesn't matter for Ferdinand's well-being. What matters is what you are like. Perhaps you were born gay; that's who you are. It shouldn't matter whether heterosexuality is the norm, or the characteristically human orientation. What counts is that individual's personality, and a gay person can thrive just as surely: by living in accordance with who he is, and so achieving self-fulfilment.

I won't try to offer a complete theory of self-fulfilment here, but philosopher L. W. Sumner may have pointed the way for happiness to figure in such a view: he defines well-being as *authentic happiness*. To be authentically happy, your happiness must be grounded in your life, and reflect who you truly are. Experience machine happiness isn't authentic, because it isn't genuinely rooted in your life. Also inauthentic is the happiness of 'happy slaves' and brainwashing victims, whose happiness reflects values that aren't genuinely their own.

The notion of authenticity may lie behind common worries about technologies for human enhancement, like 'morality pills' to make you nicer, or genetic engineering to make your children smarter: such manipulations might undermine authenticity. They might, for instance, make your actions or emotions less fully *yours*. This question could receive a lot of attention in coming decades.

Whatever else self-fulfilment involves, I would suggest it includes authentic happiness. Perhaps it also involves success in the things you care about—the values or commitments that shape your identity. Being a parent or physician, say, may be part of your identity. So you do well, in part, by succeeding in being a good parent or doctor.

Even this might not give us a complete theory of well-being, but it should be enough for us to see where happiness might fit into the larger picture. Whatever the right theory of well-being, happiness is clearly important for human flourishing.

Who's to say?

Study: New Yorkers Unhappiest People in America (Because We Work Hard and Read Books, Unlike Lazy, Stupid Hicks)

A recent headline in the *Village Voice*

The study in question did indeed suggest that people in Louisiana, and every other state, are happier than New Yorkers. Does that mean Louisianans are *better off*? Some will say yes, some no.

But no experiment can fully settle the matter, because this is a dispute about values. New Yorkers might value achievement more, while Louisianans may value enjoyment more. *Strivers* versus *enjoyers*; the ant and the grasshopper . A philosophical theory of well-being might be able to settle the question: if the right theory tells us that achievement is more important for well-being than enjoyment, then New Yorkers might stand vindicated: they are better off than the Louisianans.

But 'values' are pretty mysterious. Unlike electrons and elephants, nobody's quite sure what values are, where they come from, or whether they really exist at all. Why should we trust the opinions of philosophers spinning theories about them from the armchair? You might think there's no settling the New York/Louisiana debate. It's just a matter of opinion.

Here is a short answer, just to reduce the sceptic's fears and keep us on track: I will assume, for the purposes of this book, that values are entirely a product of the human mind. We project value onto the world. Things are actually good, bad, right, or wrong insofar as we would deem them to be so, under the right conditions.

I do not think there is a unique set of 'right' values, or that all reasonable people everywhere will fully converge on the same set of values. To some extent, the right answers will be relative to the population you're talking about. But there may yet be fairly sharp limits on the range of values that can hold up under reflection: *reflectively sustainable* values. And even if there are multiple right answers, there may be lots of unambiguously wrong answers.

For example: many people will tell you that only happiness matters. But even a moment's reflection on experience machine cases or scratchers tends to cause people to drop that opinion like a hot potato. This is some evidence that people are simply wrong to think that only happiness matters; even they don't believe it when they stop to think about it.

Or take moral opinions about the treatment of animals. Many Americans today hold something like the following constellation of opinions: eating pigs and cows from the typical supermarket is just fine; treating dogs and horses in the same manner is terribly immoral; and hunting deer is also wrong. I'm not sure what the right answers are about the ethics of meat-eating, though I am inclined to think that a diet including moderate amounts of meat from humanely treated animals is morally acceptable. Where I

89

live, to blow Bambi's brains out with a .30-06 and gnaw on his bones is positively doing the environment, and people, a favour. It may in fact be the most humane and environmentally friendly meal you'll have all year. (Growing crops kills myriad small animals, and factory farmed meat from the supermarket is an environmental, health, and humanitarian nightmare.)

You might disagree with me. No matter: I challenge the reader to reconcile the initial set of opinions. There is, I submit, no non-crazy way to make them consistent. On this issue, many people's moral attitudes are an incoherent mash of maudlin sentimentality and feeble rationalization.

Philosophical reflection can do a lot of good in cases like these, helping us to clear out the cobwebs between our ears and think more clearly and intelligently about our values. Sometimes we will converge on a single answer, as happened in the modern era, when virtually all intelligent, reflective human beings came to accept ideals of human equality. Only in enclaves trapped in the Dark Ages do we find people still convinced that slavery is OK. So there are probably some universal values owing to our common human nature, even if not all values are universal. Where disagreement seems intractable, we may simply have to admit that there is more than one set of reflectively sustainable values. Maybe neither liberals nor conservatives are wrong; perhaps both represent solutions that reasonable people can take toward the complexities of life. But that hardly means that anything goes, like fascism.

In short, making value judgements does not require us to get into anything occult or mysterious. And we can allow lots of room for relativity and plurality without becoming rank subjectivists who think anything goes. We can still maintain that some ways of living are better than others.

Chapter 7
Getting outside oneself: virtue and meaning

'Must get lonely here, J.F.'
'Not really. I *make* friends. They're toys. My friends are toys. I make them. It's a hobby. I'm a genetic designer.'

Pris and J. F. Sebastian, *Blade Runner*

Two legacies

Sometime in 1889, my great-great-grandfather Jacob Tuteur disappeared. This was unfortunate timing, as his young wife was then pregnant with their son, Edward. No one is really certain what became of Jacob; perhaps he was murdered. More likely, he simply took off and abandoned his family. (There is some evidence he spent his last days, long after, in a Texas nursing home.) That, at any rate, is what Edward believed. His bitterness at the apparent betrayal, combined with many strokes of bad luck, ultimately left two people dead, another life ruined, and many others hurt. All told, Jacob Tuteur's disappearance left a trail of suffering that spanned at least four generations. As far as his known descendants can tell, that is his sole legacy, all that is left of the man. We know nothing else of him.

Another great-great-grandfather, Billy McClure, raised the woman who would become Edward's wife, Zada. She in turn did the lion's share of bringing up my father. Billy was a self-educated man of considerable erudition, known in Southern Ohio for formidable debating skills. (What I wouldn't give for his library, which his God-fearing wife mostly consigned to the flames on his death.) He was known as well for honesty and generosity. Family legend has it that Billy could walk into any bank and get a loan on a handshake. Those qualities may have cost him the family business, a couple of general stores and a small country inn, as he apparently extended credit to too many folks who weren't able to repay him. As a result, my father was born into poverty. I do not know how much of Billy's thinking made its way into this book, though some of Zada's views can be found in the last chapter. But he left his descendants a great trove of cultural and spiritual capital, helping sustain the family through some of the same poverty and other hardships that broke Edward. Four generations of real wealth, and counting.

Neither of these men may have been particularly *happy* during their lives. But in the final reckoning, this does not appear to be the most important thing about them. More important, I think, is what they did, what they contributed. The advantages they left, or failed to leave, for those who came after. Whether they acted well, or badly.

The priority of virtue

Well-being, we saw, may not necessarily involve virtue: it may be possible for bad people, like Genghis Khan, to flourish. But this hardly means that virtue isn't important.

Not that it's a bad bet from the perspective of self-interest. Most parents seem to recognize this, and try to raise their children to be decent people, partly because they think honesty, fairness, compassion, and loyalty will serve them well. As a general rule, people don't like to hang out with untrustworthy, heartless reprobates. On the positive side, we saw in Chapter 5 that caring and doing for others tends to bring greater happiness. At any rate, most people do in fact have moral commitments: we value honesty, loyalty, kindness, and justice. To act against those values may be to make ourselves failures on our own terms. For most people, a life of immorality probably tends to exact a high price.

Still, there is no guarantee that immorality won't sometimes make a person happier, or even better off. Nor that the bad person won't do pretty well, at least by conventional standards. Aristotelians and others convinced of the intrinsic benefits of virtue tend to find such concessions worrisome. Sometimes, it seems, the concern is that we can't take virtue or morality seriously enough if we admit that people can profit from immorality. But that doesn't follow at all. In fact very few serious thinkers fail to give virtue pride of place in thinking about the good life.

Virtually all ethical philosophers agree on something we might call the *priority of virtue*: broadly and crudely speaking, the demands of virtue trump all other values in life. Acting badly is out of the question, even if that would make us happier or otherwise benefit us. This is basically a consensus position in philosophy, though of course philosophers disagree about what virtue involves. For the great majority, it includes acting morally, and even apparent exceptions tend not to advocate acting badly. Nietzsche, for instance, was no fan of conventional morality, but he did not counsel against living admirably. And many philosophers would allow that nonmoral reasons sometimes outweigh moral reasons. If you discover that keeping your promise to meet some friends at the movies will mean losing your job, it's OK to break the promise. But, at the very least, we must not act badly.

The ancient debate over whether virtue necessarily benefits us is interesting, but it can also be somewhat of a red herring. Whether it benefits us or not, most parties can agree that virtue, including morality, is our top priority.

A right to be happy?

All this talk of 'virtue' can seem a bit dry. So let's pause to consider what it means for the pursuit of happiness. Obviously, acting badly in the name of happiness is out of the question. Here's one way that can play out.

'I have a right to be happy.' On hearing these words, one may want to duck: what follows is rarely good news. When someone says something like this, it tends to be so transparently aimed at rationalizing some sort of seedy behaviour that we aren't likely to take it seriously. Yet the claim is often heard all the same, at least in these parts. Is there anything to it?

In a word: no. No one has a right to be happy. Such a right is nowhere to be found in the American Declaration of Independence, which speaks only of its pursuit. And few philosophers have ever posited a right to be happy.

Let me qualify that a bit. If one means 'I have a right to be happy' in the same sense that one says 'I have a right to chew gum', then of course we have a right to be happy. Nothing wrong with being happy. But that's not what people mean when they say this: rather, they mean it in the same sense that one tells the boss, 'I have a right to get paid', after fulfilling the terms of employment. The person is claiming an entitlement to happiness: something he deserves, and which the world, or someone, owes him.

It is questionable whether anyone deserves much of anything, except to be treated with respect. Be that as it may, the idea that happiness is owed to anyone is deeply implausible, and few serious thinkers have claimed any such thing. A right to the necessities of happiness, perhaps, but not a right actually to be happy.

The mistaken assertion of a right to be happy is an example of a broader error, namely a belief in cosmic entitlements. For instance, that one deserves a reward merely for being virtuous. Not from anyone in particular, just...the world. A common reply to any mention of environmental concerns, for instance, goes something like this: 'I work hard, so I deserve to have nice things.' Perhaps there's genuinely nothing wrong with, say, an Arizona homeowner purchasing an extremely wasteful watering system for her lush desert lawn. But the idea that the individual *deserves* it is not terribly compelling. For most of us, hard work is a given, not something we get a prize for.

Life is not fair. Some people, through no fault of their own, will fail to find happiness. Some will be stuck in marriages that don't make them happy, yet aren't bad enough to justify putting their children through a divorce. Just as others, too young, drop dead from a heart attack. No one is entitled to be happy. But even the unalterably unhappy may still lead good lives, and many of them do. We will return to this in the final chapter.

Another kind of mistake: it is possible to make too much use of the rights one actually has. A man buys a piece of land, for example, then ignores the neighbours' pleas and proceeds to build a monstrous house that blocks a prized view from nearby businesses, driving away customers and otherwise annoying everyone around him. Much of the time he operates noisy machinery that shatters the peaceful environment that drew many other residents to the area. As a result, some of the neighbours have put their homes or businesses up for sale.

The reader knows exactly what the man said in response to his neighbours' entreaties: 'I have a right to do what I want with my property.'

This is a curious justification. The man may well be correct about his rights. He may have violated no legal code. Nor perhaps was anyone morally entitled to prevent him from doing it, or to exact compensation from him. At any rate, the man is calling on a perfectly ordinary understanding of rights. Let's grant him his view, then, and concede that he indeed acted within his rights in building his beastly abode. Is that any defence?

Consider a brief list of some of your rights, so understood. You have a right not to visit your wife in the hospital. You have a right to be callous, insensitive, and inconsiderate. You have the right to annoy everyone around you. You have the right to tell your kindly grandmother she looks like the back end of a mule. You may have the right to let your neighbour starve, though you have food enough to share. You have, in short, the right to be a deplorable, despicable, contemptible jerk. You have the right to be a terrible person and lead a terrible life. But of course you wouldn't be *justified* in doing any of these things.

What makes living with each other bearable, and civilization possible, is the willingness of all parties to *limit the exercise of their rights*. Arguably, to invoke a right to do something is merely to declare that others may not forcibly stop you from doing it, or demand recompense after the fact. Obviously, if the only constraint we put on our behaviour is to avoid doing things that might warrant the use of force or compensatory proceedings against us, life will rapidly become, as the English philosopher Thomas Hobbes (1588–1679) might have said, 'nasty, brutish and short'. A society in which 'I have a right to' counts as a justification for doing something is in deep trouble.

Perhaps because this sort of thing has become somewhat of a problem, contemporary English vernacular has a special name for people who act as badly as they have a right to, and it has become quite popular. They may do no one strictly an injustice, paying all their bills, telling no lies, and so forth. They might even be, otherwise, good people. But they are very inconsiderate, and very hard to live with. We call such people assholes.

One should not be an asshole in the pursuit of happiness.

Meaning: connecting with what matters

A puzzle

I've been stressing the importance of morality, but acting and living well goes far beyond moral goodness. We don't just admire people for being good, but also for exercising such homely virtues as friendliness, wit, or resilience. Or, simply being skilled in the art of living. 'She really knows how to live' is a pretty high compliment. Growing up, one of the harsher criticisms we could receive was that we were acting soft, weak, spoiled—unable to handle our business. Or, half-jokingly, 'You're not worth the powder it'd take to blow you up.'

Another crucial part of living well has to do with *meaning*: very roughly, connecting with people and things that matter. We want not just to be happy, or good. We also want to pass our lives in meaningful, worthwhile pursuits. We've seen that such activities can make us happier. But beyond that, they are simply worth doing, quite apart from the happiness they bring.

In recent years the question of a meaningful life has become especially interesting to people with children. The reason? According to some studies, having kids doesn't make us happier. It may even be a downer. These studies seem to have hit a nerve with many parents, who are not generally keen to think that their darling spawn have made their lives worse. For years we've been clubbing our childless friends over the head with tales of the delights of parenting, so this is a little embarrassing.

Now those studies could be wrong, and some researchers claim they are. But they probably aren't *that* wrong. At least, not in this part of the world. (It might take a village to raise a child, but many folks have little more than an under-rested spouse, if that, to help keep the little ones entertained, loved, disciplined, clothed, and fed.) A lot of parents were happier when they could just go out for a drink at night, and also didn't need one. Still, those of us with kids can't shake the conviction that our lives are *much* better for it—happier or not. Either we are in the grip of an unshakeable delusion, or kids benefit us in some other way than just making us happy. What could that be? An obvious thought is that they contribute a great deal of meaning to our lives. Let's see what this involves.

The roots of meaning: appreciating versus liking

The importance of relationships and activity for happiness, we saw, reflects our status as social creatures and as agents: lovers, and doers. The importance of meaning for happiness reflects a third aspect of human nature: we are also *valuers*. We do not just want or like things, like dogs do; we also value things. To value something is to see it as mattering, as something you ought to want: as grounding reasons for you to respond to it in certain ways. For example, you probably don't just prefer to be a person of integrity. You value integrity. Which means you see integrity as something you should maintain—not simply because you like it, but because it is worth maintaining. When you fall short and sacrifice some of your integrity, you don't just feel frustrated. You feel ashamed or guilty: you failed to measure up.

You can want or like something without valuing it. A smoker trying to quit may yet want a cigarette, but regard herself as having no reason at all to want one, or to smoke one. Or: I like Cheez Whiz. (A uranium-yellow synthetic spray 'cheese' in an aerosol can.) It tastes good to me, but the pleasure of it is a cheap, meaningless pleasure. I don't see Cheez Whiz as particularly deserving of my appetites. It would never occur to me to try to get someone else to appreciate it. *I* don't even appreciate it. I just like it, the same way my mutt likes his kibbles. It's junk food.

But then I sit down to a meal of some outstanding barbecue. To pull this sort of meal off, I realize, is no easy feat. The preparation is subtle, clearly the work of a talented cook. I like the ribs, yes. But I also *appreciate* them, as well as the artistry of the chef. To feed this creation to my dog, who cannot appreciate it and might at best regard it as a really tasty kibble, would be scandalous. I might try to explain the virtues of this preparation to a friend who's a newcomer to barbecue, hoping she too will come to appreciate it as I do. This is not just pleasant but a rewarding, satisfying meal. All the more so if shared in good company.

While we don't usually talk about dinner as a meaningful experience, neither would we consider such a repast to be a cheap, meaningless pleasure. (There's a reason Jesus wrapped up his life with a meal, and it wasn't The Last Drive-Through.) It is pretty meaningful to have the privilege of sharing a well-executed meal in good company.

The difference between *appreciating* and *liking* marks a critical difference between human and merely animal enjoyments, between the fulfilling and the merely pleasant. In appreciating things, we experience them as valuable, as mattering and worth wanting. We do not merely feel good about them, the way a dog likes his chow. Appreciation, we will see, appears to be central to a meaningful life.

Meaning in life, subjective and objective

Let's begin with the subjective side of meaning: feeling like your life is meaningful. Seeing your life as meaningful, I would suggest, involves *appreciative engagement with what you see as having merit or worth*. Any kind of excellence or beauty, for example, or simply the intrinsic worth that a human being has. To put it in plainer language, our lives seem meaningful to us when it feels like we're engaged with people and things that matter. Our lives feel worthwhile to us. This is a bit loose and could use further argument, but it should be good enough for our purposes.

To illustrate: Stephen Darwall, a philosopher whose work strongly influences me here, offers the example of Daniel Golub, a concert pianist who is rapturously lost in his virtuoso performance of a

13. Keith Richards of The Rolling Stones

great piece. That is a model of appreciative engagement with merit: he recognizes the excellence of the music and the performance, and takes joy in connecting with those values. Such experiences are highly meaningful. Personally, I prefer this example (Figure 13):

Suppose your life *feels* meaningful to you. Does that mean it really is meaningful? Imagine you're a demented monarch who takes great satisfaction in carrying out absurd and cruel policies that strike you as really important. From your perspective, you're connecting with things that matter. Could this be a meaningful life? Philosophers divide on this question, but it seems a little extreme to call such a life utterly meaningless. Even if your goals are completely worthless, they still seem meaningful to you. So why should we insist that your life has no meaning at all? Subjective meaning probably counts for something.

Still, wouldn't your life be a lot more meaningful if you were engaged with things that actually did matter? Part of a meaningful life is just doing things that are in fact worthwhile. When people cite Martin Luther King or Mother Teresa as exemplars of meaningful lives, they probably aren't thinking about how it seemed to those individuals. Rather, the mere fact that they devoted their lives to great accomplishments makes them meaningful. Any life dedicated to worthwhile ends is meaningful.

So meaning can arise both from connecting with what seems valuable to you, and from connecting with what is actually valuable. Call these *subjective* and *objective* meaning, respectively. The most meaningful lives will combine subjective and objective meaning. In the central case of meaning, then, *what makes life meaningful is appreciative engagement with merit or worth*. Philosopher Susan Wolf makes a similar point when she writes that 'meaning arises when subjective attraction meets objective attractiveness'. Lives can have some meaning without the subjective component, say when we do good things without really appreciating their value. Likewise without the objective aspect, as when we are deluded about the worth of our activities. But the meaningfulness of our lives is diminished when either component is missing.

Why meaning matters

It seems obviously important to lead a meaningful life. But it is not so obvious *why*. How does meaning make our lives better? We saw in Chapter 5 that meaningful activity is a major source of happiness. In fact I suspect that our lives can only be emotionally fulfilling when they seem meaningful to us. We might think of emotional fulfilment as a mixture of joy and attunement that arises when we appreciatively engage with what we see as valuable. Joy, due to the recognition of good things happening and being connected with them. And attunement, due to the recognition that one is doing, or being, what one ought: a sense of completion or, well, fulfilment. It is not clear how you could achieve this state without feeling like your life is fairly meaningful.

Still, meaningful pursuits do not always make us happier. Sometimes they are difficult and stressful. An artist, researcher, or politician might lead a highly meaningful life, yet not be particularly happy. And then there are the children: they don't always make us happier, even as they add meaning to our lives. How, then, do we benefit?

One possibility is that the experience of meaning just is a good experience to have. Not just because it involves pleasure, but simply as a positive experience in its own right. Perhaps an experience can benefit us either by being pleasant, or by being meaningful or rewarding.

A more familiar thought is that meaningful lives tend to be more *successful*. In doing things we find meaningful, we achieve a measure of success in things we care about. Being a good father or friend. Helping others, creating beauty, or pushing the boundaries of human knowledge or athletic achievement. Such successes seem to make our lives go better for us, quite apart from any happiness payoff.

Finally, even when meaningful pursuits don't benefit us, they can still be worthwhile. Many a political dissident has paid a steep price for their efforts, and some no doubt would have been better off doing something else. But their struggles may add greatly to the meaningfulness of their lives, benefit or no, simply because they have so much merit.

Summing up: if I am right, then *a major part of the good life is connecting with what really matters*. This contributes centrally to making our lives fulfilling, meaningful, and worthwhile. Variants of this ideal probably arise in all the major religions. Saint Thomas Aquinas, for instance, saw the human ideal as union with God—the beatific vision. Our goal, in essence, is to connect as closely as possible with the good.

Meaning and modern life: appreciators and consumers

Let's see how these points might apply to our everyday lives. The ideal of connection is radically different from the ideal of simply getting whatever you happen to want, perhaps the standard view among moderns since Hobbes. In the picture we've been discussing, which Darwall traces to Aristotle, humans are valuers who seek to connect with the things they ought to desire. The world's value does not simply depend on our whims, but is something we discover. We remind ourselves to keep our eye on the ball, not letting our desires become detached from the things that really matter. And we educate and cultivate ourselves, in part so that we may better appreciate the worth of things, enriching our lives in the process. In short, the ideal of connection counsels us to seek a life of appreciative engagement with value: to be an *appreciator*, as we might call it.

In the Hobbesian view, reflected in mainstream economics, we are brute desirers who wish simply to get our fill. Or at least to keep the pangs of hunger at bay—*Homo gastropodus*, a stomach with legs. Like clever dogs chasing ever more kibble, we treat our desires as simply a given, not something to be scrutinized, reflected upon, and improved. The Hobbesian sees the world as something to be used and consumed, its value depending wholly on the individual's whims. You don't connect with other people; you contract. Or, if you're a demented genetic designer like *Blade*

Runner's Sebastian, you synthesize. Appreciation doesn't enter into it; you just *want*. The familiar term for this beast is 'consumer'.

I first began distinguishing consumers and appreciators in my years at a vacation spot, where I noticed a divide in the way tourists approached the place. Many, the appreciators, arrived with an open mind, adapted themselves to where they were, and enjoyed the place for what it was. Others, the consumers—'touroids' was the local term—seemed to regard the locale simply as something to amuse or entertain them. 'What, no miniature golf?' 'Why can't I get a decent cappuccino around here?' 'I'm bored, there's nothing to do here.' Never mind that they were in one of the most beautiful locations on the planet. Family burial plots were routinely trampled in search of a quaint photograph, 'no trespassing' signs notwithstanding. To see what I mean, observe some vacationers at another spot in Figure 14 as they extract souvenir photos from Buddhist monks taking their daily walk.

Few things, I suspect, can more thoroughly drain life of meaning, dignity, or joy than having this sort of outlook. It is better to be an appreciator than a consumer.

14. Tourists photographing monks, Luang Prabang, Laos

Luckily, few people have fully embraced the grim Hobbesian perspective in their lives. Connecting with value happens in our work, sports, the arts, nature, and other encounters with beauty, hobbies, good works, and most of all our connections with other people. In fact, probably most activities we like to do confer some meaning. In a market economy, most paid work is worthwhile and meaningful to some degree, as long as your dealings are honest. One of the more meaningful episodes of my youth was simply earning a paycheck and paying the bills. At age 16, I packed up and went to another state, where I rented a bed for the summer and paid my expenses clearing tables in a restaurant. Just providing for yourself is a pretty meaningful act. If you sell shoes, you're not only providing for yourself and your family, but also offering a valued service to your employer and your customers. Your paycheck reflects the value you provide for others. All this is worthwhile and meaningful. (Admittedly, in many jobs the *sense* of meaning may be fairly weak, since the fruits of your labour may be pretty far removed from your daily experience.)

Similarly, you might see something to admire in a well-played game of football, and so find playing it to be meaningful and fulfilling. You might find just *watching* football on television to be fulfilling, if in so doing you are not just having fun but appreciating the skill of the athletes. Is this any different from appreciating a ballet or opera? Naturally, actually doing the activity tends to be more fulfilling than merely appreciating someone else's performance of it. We can participate both as agent and observer.

Perhaps the most important form of appreciative engagement is *social* engagement: talking and doing things together. Doing things for others. Unless you are a psychopath, you cannot help but see value in other people and in responding appropriately to them. Indeed, people may seem to most of us to be the *chief* source of value. Given the complexity of human sociality, our interactions with each other demand tremendous sensitivity, discernment, skill, and sophistication. If it doesn't always seem that way, it's because humans are so good at it. Even something as basic as good conversation is an art, requiring considerable intelligence and practice.

Just hanging out with friends can be highly meaningful and fulfilling. Doing things for them, even more so. Since the great majority of people have social lives, this suggests that one need not pursue great accomplishment to lead a perfectly meaningful, fulfilling life. It may be that few people truly fit the stereotype of the mindless consumer leading an empty, meaningless life.

Summing up: the place of happiness in a good life

I cannot confidently enumerate all the values that factor into a good life. But I have suggested that happiness is part, but not the whole, of human well-being. Beyond well-being, it is still more important to act well: virtue is our first priority in life. Leading a meaningful life contributes both to well-being and to virtue.

Does this mean happiness isn't important? Of course not. Health isn't the only thing that matters either, but no one denies the importance of health. Recall our fictional communities, Eudonia and Maldonia, from Chapter 4: would you consider it unimportant which community you lived in? Happiness isn't everything, but still it matters—rather a lot. A society that resembles Maldonia has some pretty grave defects.

This chapter and the last have emphasized how distinct the elements of a good life are: happiness, morality, and so forth. Sometimes they can pull in different directions. But for the most part they do not. By and large, the ways of living that bring happiness also tend, by any reasonable measure, to be *good* ways of living.

Consider the young woman pictured in Figure 15. Just from looking at a photograph, we cannot be certain that she is happy, or

15. A young Tibetan woman

a good person. But I suspect she strikes *you* as happy, and good. As a general rule, people who are selfish, shallow, or mean do not look like this. For the most part, I think, they do not look happy at all.

Dr Thomas Mettee, a family practitioner in Cleveland, Ohio, was one of the happiest-seeming men I have known. As with very many of the happiest people I've met—all of them, actually—much of his happiness derived from his concern for others. Indeed, leading a life of service to others. When he walked into a room, everyone's spirits lifted. He could have you laughing on your deathbed.

Mettee saw what was unique in each patient, and he seemed instinctively to know what you needed, what needed to be said. He could deliver a stern lecture on the necessity of losing weight, or quitting smoking, and not make you feel defensive in the least. He recognized that families need care and wise counsel just as much as the patients, and I am sure he helped to keep many families working together through the hardest passages of life. Nightly house calls, if called for. If need be, he would bend the rules to get a patient what she needed, perhaps commandeering some hospital equipment to allow her to die at home, in her own bed. If a patient had a favourite flower, he might place it on her chest in her final minutes, the petals rising and falling with her slackening breath. When the blossom ceased to move, the gathered family would know that she had passed on.

Three nights ago Dr Tom himself passed away, I hope in the care of one of the many physicians he trained. Though it is only February, the flowers he sent for our garden—daffodils, my mother's favourite, and tulips, my father's—have already begun peeking up through the soil.

Chapter 8
A good life

'Yes, we're happy…We could all use a little more money, but
we have what we need, and what we don't have, God takes care of.'
'What would you do if you had more money?'
'Probably buy bigger houses…But on the other hand, we probably
wouldn't meet like this every afternoon. So, maybe not.'

> Three women sitting on cement blocks in front of their
> houses, Monterrey, Mexico. Average household income,
> 'perhaps $500 per month'. From Dan Buettner, *Thrive*

What makes for a good life?

To put the pursuit of happiness in its proper context, we need
some notion of what a good life looks like. One of the more
noteworthy features of a good life is that, like a good play or a
pleasant visit from the in-laws, it eventually draws to a conclusion:
you die. This is probably not something you are looking forward
to, but neither is it such a terrible thing. If the old never died, the
young would soon find things pretty crowded, and get really tired
of hearing the same stories over and over again. And if you alone
gained immortality, you would soon find things pretty lonely and
weird, as the world leaves you behind. We don't know what
happens when we die, but I suspect you aren't planning to end up

someplace uncomfortably warm. If there's no afterlife at all, then it's going to be pretty much like it was before you were born. That wasn't so bad, was it?

Before your time comes, you may look back on a long life and take stock. Did you have a good life? This is the really important question, the one you really want to get right. But how can you tell? What counts as a good life?

It is surprisingly hard to define a good life. Or maybe not so surprising. But let me venture a suggestion. I'm not sure it's correct; in fact I'm not aware of many similar discussions in the literature, so these waters are not as well-charted as one might expect. But it seems a reasonable starting point.

Let's say that a good life is a life you could reasonably affirm. Put another way, *a good life is a life that you could justifiably be satisfied with.* (I am being brief here, leaving a more detailed argument for another time.) Call this a 'justified affirmation' account of the good life.

There may be other reasonable ways to think about 'good lives', serving different purposes. When setting goals for oneself, or one's government, it may make sense to focus on a more demanding notion of the good life: a life worth aspiring to. This would be a 'justified aspiration' notion of the good life.

Here, though, I am interested in the way we evaluate lives as they are lived, or when looking back on them. The question is, when are we justified in affirming, or being satisfied with, our lives? As the last two chapters explained, there seem to be at least two fundamental parts to a good life: whether your life is good *for* you, and whether the way you lead it is good. Well-being, and virtue.

We saw in Chapter 3 that it may not be very important whether you are *actually* satisfied with your life. But here the question is whether you have reason to be satisfied with your life. Whether you *could* reasonably take such an attitude. This is a question about how your life measures up, not your state of mind. And that could be important even if it doesn't matter so much whether you actually do have the attitude.

Interestingly, for your life to be good for you, it does not have to go well for you; you don't need to fare well, or do well. You don't need a high level of well-being. Your life just needs to be a good thing for you to have had. For this, it may suffice if your life is *worth living* for you: better than having not lived. But this seems a bit weak: a life just barely worth living seems at best to be okay, acceptable, or maybe tolerable. So let's say, to count as a genuine good for you, your life has to be *well* worth living for you: substantially better than having not lived. This is vague, but we shouldn't expect precision here.

So one part of the good life concerns your *well-being*. The other part, very roughly, is the ethical part of it, or *virtue*. Have you conducted yourself well? Have you chosen and acted well? Choosing and living well isn't just a moral thing: it's more broadly a matter of living sensibly and wisely. This might include being prudent in your personal affairs, maintaining your dignity, getting the most out of life, and so forth. If you live very well, we might say you lived *admirably*.

All that said, morality is clearly the most important part of the picture, and the most important thing to get right in a good life. We already saw this in Chapter 7, but let's examine the point a bit closer. In thinking about good lives, it can be helpful to apply the 'eulogy test': imagine you're delivering the eulogy for a person. Make it a dry run to an empty room so you don't have to worry about offending anyone. Would you say that he had a good life?

As a general rule, people tend not to say that bad people had good lives. If you think so-and-so was a moral degenerate who treated

A good life

111

people like dirt, you are not very likely to think of him as having had a good life. Even if he were wealthy, happy, and admired by many, having essentially got away with being a horrible person.

On the flip side, think of someone you consider to have been a really good person, who conducted her life courageously, kindly, justly, and in an otherwise morally admirable way. Most likely, you would also deem her to have had a good life. Abraham Lincoln and Winston Churchill suffered greatly from depression. Martin Luther King, Jr., was murdered at age 39 after a not particularly cushy career leading the civil rights movement. During the prime of his life, Nelson Mandela spent 27 years in prison. None of them had particularly enviable lives. Yet these are the sorts of people who tend to get cited as *paradigms* of good lives.

When we talk of good lives, are we just talking about *morally* good or virtuous lives? Certainly not. Think again of the eulogy test: is it not relevant, when summing up a person's life, whether she enjoyed it? Whether she was happy, or miserable? Whether she succeeded or failed in her important goals? Mandela seems to have had a good life, at least given the standard narrative of things. But the fact that he spent nearly three decades in a prison cell, after which his marriage crumbled, at least prompts one to pause and think about it. It would have been an even better life had he been able to accomplish great things without so much suffering.

Now imagine a very kind, courageous, and honourable person who does good works for others, but endures an endless stream of horrors: excruciating illnesses, ostracism, and public humiliation. Watching her children die one by one. A lifelong depression that frequently leaves her contemplating suicide. And an early, lonely, painful death. So few were the consolations of this life that she would rather never have been born. Her goodness as a person counts for a lot, yet it would be hard to call this a good life. On the contrary, it sounds like a very undesirable life, a life one would be hard-pressed to affirm.

A good life may not require doing or faring well. But it seems one must do well enough to make life well worth living. And most of all, it requires acting reasonably well. A good life is a life well-lived, and well worth living.

Prospects for a good life

There is a happy moral to this account of the good life: the good life is not hard to get. The well-being side of the equation, after all, is very undemanding. Even the average Charlie Brown, for whom things rarely go well, can still have a life well worth living. Most of the time, life is awash in small pleasures: almost every hour brings pleasant smells, pleasing sights and sounds, agreeable sensations, amusing thoughts. This is not always so obvious, because we are so used to it, and because we are wired to respond more strongly to the bad things. (This is called 'negativity bias'.)

Yes, there are times when the suffering overwhelmingly trumps the pleasures. Indeed when no consciousness at all might be preferable. For some periods, life may be such that it genuinely wouldn't be worth living, if that's all the future could bring. Yet no one reaches old age and lies on his deathbed thinking, 'if only I had killed myself when I was 17. Suicide really was the answer.' I've not heard of it, anyway. Eventually the pain subsides, age mellows us and gives us a better sense of proportion, and we realize how good it is to be alive.

Since the well-being part of a good life is so easily met, the chief obstacle to a good life, for most of us, is our own choices. We are far more likely to undermine our lives by acting badly than by being unhappy or unsuccessful. If you do badly by your family, cheat people, are selfish or just plain mean, you will have a much harder time saying honestly that you're satisfied with your life.

The other side of this, though, is that *the most important element of a good life is wholly in your control*: it is your choice whether to act well. For the most part, whether you have a good life is up to you. You may or may not find happiness. But you can handle life's slings and arrows with goodness, dignity, and grace.

I would suggest that most people do, and consequently have good lives: lives worthy of affirmation. This may be the real lesson of the high rates of reported life satisfaction around the world: perhaps most people are satisfied with their lives because they have good *reason* to be. It does not mean they are happy or even doing well. It just means they recognize their lives to be good, and appreciate it. If anything, perhaps *more* people should be satisfied with their lives. Maybe many people fail to recognize how good their lives really are.

So most people have lives well worth living, and arguably conduct themselves reasonably well: mostly doing right by their families and friends, honouring their debts, earning an honest living, fulfilling their obligations—leading decent, dignified lives. Even those hobbled by severe disabilities can choose to handle them well. They may also bring joy, meaning, and inspiration into the lives of those around them. However modest your achievements, you can take satisfaction in knowing that you handled your responsibilities, knew something of love, and took in a bit of Earth's, and humankind's, splendour.

For my own part, most of the good lives that come to mind involve average folks leading pretty ordinary lives. (Though if you think about it, even the most ordinary human life is a pretty extraordinary thing.) In fact good lives may be inversely correlated with accomplishment and fame: notoriety and extraordinary achievements tend to require a single-minded devotion that can compromise more fundamental elements of a good life, like family relationships. I've met a good number of accomplished people, very impressive in their fields. But more than a few of them have come across as pretty unimpressive human beings, whose families I do not envy.

The homemaker who shepherded her family over the decades with discernment, sensitivity, wisdom, patience, and a sharp wit may pass unremarked by the wider world. But I would much prefer that my children go on to lead lives like hers than Woolf's, Wittgenstein's, Van Gogh's, or Hemingway's. Those of us observing from a safe distance should be glad of the great men and women whose fruits we enjoy. But that doesn't mean we should want to live like them.

Setting priorities

Knowing the criteria for a good life is a far cry from knowing how to get there. So how does one put the claims made in this book into practice? What does our discussion suggest about what our priorities should be?

There's really no general answer to this question, because each of us has different problems and different needs. Anyway, I have no expertise in advising people about their lives. Still, it seems a waste to have come this far and not at least have a conversation about what our priorities ought to be. Each of us is different, but not that different. All human beings face a lot of similar problems, and have a lot of similar needs. Many of our values are common, as well. Consider how you can become friends with people in any part of the world, and how we can all enjoy many of the same stories and films. Nobody watches *Star Wars* and thinks Darth Vader is a really terrific guy.

So here, for what it's worth, are a few suggestions on the most important items to bear in mind—areas where it is easy to make mistakes that make your life worse. They will not apply to all persons at all times, but they might apply to most. While these reflections draw on my philosophical training and knowledge of the scientific literature, it is not expert counsel, nor will I offer any real argument for the list. These are just suggestions, based on my sense of where the most significant practical concerns lie. You'll

likely have your own ideas in these matters, perhaps better suited
to your personality and circumstances.

What sort of list would you offer to a friend, sibling, or child trying
to decide how to live?

Connect with people and things that matter

> Someday, someday, but certainly not now, I'd like to learn how to
> have a conversation.
>
> A 16-year-old boy who relies heavily on texting

This, we saw earlier, is both a key source of happiness and,
independently, an important part of living well. Especially today,
when so many forces try to get us absorbed in trivia, it is easy to
devote far too many of one's waking hours to things that aren't
worthwhile or important. Family and friends are the obvious case
here, but beauty, excellence, and other forms of worth are all major
sources of meaning in our lives. And failing to engage enough with
them is the sort of thing we are all too likely to recognize at funerals.

I once spent some time with a deeply unhappy, fractured family
who displayed all the signs of a materialistic lifestyle. Work was
about making as much money as possible. That money was spent
on fancy cars and other markers of status. Shopping was one of
their main leisure activities, with one young woman describing
herself as a 'shopping addict'. Most of the family seemed lost
talking about anything they regarded as very important, or having
any real substance at all. Deep or meaningful conversation was
apparently not a regular feature of their lives. They seemed
isolated from one another, locked in their own private worlds.

Yet they were nice, likable people whose core values seemed
perfectly healthy, and little different from anyone else's. They
cared deeply about their family and other relationships, and there
is little doubt that they valued familiar virtues like honesty,

fairness, kindness, and loyalty. They treasured memories of personal achievements, shared experiences, and other meaningful episodes in their lives.

Most likely, they were simply pursuing the kinds of goals that their culture validated and made readily available to them. Perhaps it never occurred to them that there were viable, honourable alternatives to the single-minded pursuit of money, stuff, and status. And so they pursued a way of life that served their appetites, but undermined the things they actually cared about. The experience left me disheartened to be part of a culture that lets people down so profoundly, urging us to put our lives so thoroughly at odds with our own values.

Materialism is one threat to connection; perpetual distraction is another. As I write, we are just a decade or two into a new era of potentially nonstop artificial stimulation: cell phones, texting, handheld video games, home gaming consoles, iPads, iPods, iPhones, Facebook, Twitter, the internet, and probably a bunch of other stuff I'm forgetting. I enjoy using many of these technologies, which are popular for a reason. Sometimes they enhance our relationships, for instance helping us keep in touch with distant friends and relatives.

But they also serve less rewarding ends, and can be more than a little addictive. Having an iPhone at your disposal is like hanging a sack of doughnuts and chocolates around your neck. Yes, you *can* moderate your consumption to a healthy level. But there's a good chance you won't. The next thing you know you're texting friends from Mom's funeral, eating your dinners with headphones on, waking at night to check your Facebook feed, and playing Call of Duty at the beach. The modern day lotus eater, insensible to the call of reality.

At the limit: no reflection, no peace, and no genuinely human interactions. Maybe textual simulacra thereof, which have their

117

consolations but resemble actual face-to-face conversations roughly as much as a stick-figure drawing resembles the Mona Lisa. Soon, you may pretty much forget how to talk, as many of us already have. (This becomes starkly apparent when you visit a place where the art of conversation still thrives, like a working-class English pub.)

You can now be plugged in, but disconnected from nearly everything of worth, for every waking moment of the day. I don't know how serious a worry this is long-term. I suspect people will adjust by developing norms and habits to help them keep the technology from stripping away the fabric of their lives and rewiring their brains, leaving them incapable of functioning without constant electronic input. But there's plainly a risk of overdoing it.

A more traditional threat to connection relates to one's choice of occupation. When choosing a line of work, the temptation to go for money and status can be powerful. Particularly if you don't

16. Mealtime with the plugged-in family

have a clear idea what you want to do for a living. However, the first thing to notice is that no one gives a young graduate, who doesn't know a hawk from a handsaw, a big heap of money without extracting a pound of flesh. Those lucrative entry-level jobs in finance, law, or whatever pay a lot because, well, they *have* to pay a lot. No one in their right mind would volunteer to spend 80 hours a week toiling at an unfulfilling job in a semi-abusive environment unless they were either very desperate or very well-paid. Engineers may be among the exceptions to this rule, since they graduate with significant work skills; but then they already made a flesh donation in college.

Short of thievery or dumb luck, like having the right golfing buddies, there seem to be two paths to riches: working really hard in a punishing profession that pays well because no one would do it otherwise (e.g., law), and working really hard at something you are really good at and passionate about (e.g., Steve Jobs). At least, it's hard to imagine how else a functioning market economy could go about allocating the highest salaries. Why put people at the top of the pay scale to kick back and do something easy and fun?

If you're going for money, you'd probably best be in the 'passionate and talented' category or you're not likely to be very happy or have a very meaningful work experience. And if you are one of those individuals, it probably won't truly be the money that's motivating you, but the work itself and the idea of doing it well. The money may primarily be a sign that you're really good at what you do.

But if you're in a position to be able to choose a lucrative career, why should the money be important in the first place? Just having that option makes you a very lucky person who is unlikely to end up in the poor house no matter what you choose to do, unless it's poetry or jazz.

Recall that in the United States, household incomes above $75,000 seem on average to have zero effect on happiness. Based on the findings of a major employment study from 2009–10, this income is less than the average for the *worst-paid* college majors at mid-career, assuming your household has two working partners with similar earnings. Two experienced graduates in social work or elementary education earned, on average, a combined mid-career salary of about $80,000. Moreover, unemployment rates tended not to vary wildly across college majors—the highest mid-career rates, for architecture and linguistics, ran about 9 to 10 per cent. Those 'low-paid' social work and teaching jobs nonetheless sported decent job security in the survey: elementary educators had among the lowest mid-career unemployment rates, at 3.4 per cent, with social workers at 5.8 per cent. Which is to say that *every* college major—yes, even philosophy—tended to get decent-paying jobs, putting their income above the threshold of minimal returns, happiness-wise. Now these numbers hail from a certain time and place, and this is only a single study. Your prospects may be different. But they do suggest caution in placing a great deal of weight on the financial side of career decisions.

This is not to say that we should be indifferent to the financial side of our work choices. 'Follow your bliss' can be excellent advice, but your spouse won't be so pleased if your bliss involves not being able to pay the bills. Social workers are pretty close to the threshold where money starts to have a significant impact on happiness, and some will fall below the average or live in expensive areas. And even if money troubles don't diminish their happiness they may still have difficulty with things like getting their kids into good schools, weathering unexpected troubles like medical emergencies, or saving for retirement.

There are good reasons to prefer higher-paying jobs, even out of college. But from the happiness perspective, at least, the average person's monetary needs seem to be pretty modest, and easily met by most careers requiring college degrees in the United States.

More money has distinct advantages, but you probably won't suffer without it.

All this is by way of saying: it is foolish to let the pursuit of wealth, status, and stuff get in the way of a fulfilling, rewarding work life. If the pursuit of ambitious material goals seriously compromises your ability to connect with people and things that matter, you've likely made a big mistake.

Relax

'Laurie says Ravioli is too busy to play.'

> Three-year-old New Yorker Olivia, about her imaginary
> playmate Charlie Ravioli, who is usually too busy to play,
> and his personal assistant, Laurie

Several years back I read an interview with a Mexican businessman whose family had lived in the United States for ten years before returning to live in Merida, reputed to be a lovely city. Both countries have their pros and cons, he said, but he preferred Mexico for himself. Asked if he had any advice for his northerly neighbours, he offered one suggestion: 'Chill!'

Mexican-style laid back is certainly not for everyone; among other things, it comes at the cost of efficiency. This is very much an area where personalities, cultures, and tastes can legitimately differ. But even those who prefer a faster pace of life can try to give themselves a bit of breathing room—some time to slow down, reflect, and recharge. Or, at the very least, to notice things.

On the face of it this point may seem in tension with the idea of connection, and indeed it can be. One way to connect with things of value is to engage in challenging, meaningful work. This can sometimes leave little time to relax. In many cases the tradeoff is worth it, say because the work seems especially meaningful or

121

worthwhile. But it is always a tradeoff, because humans aren't built to always be on 'go'.

For those who have never strayed far from the fast lane, it can be hard to believe how little it is possible to do without getting bored. Our hunter-gatherer ancestors may have had 'work weeks' of fewer than 20 hours, if their present-day counterparts are any guide. (Not that hunting is exactly drudgery for them.) For most of human history, just hanging around and basically doing nothing has probably been a prominent feature of daily life. This may strike you as excruciatingly dull, and again there's nothing unreasonable about preferring a faster pace of life. On the matter of boredom, I've put the question to two trusted acquaintances who've spent a good deal of time with hunters leading traditional lifestyles, and neither saw evidence of it. One, surprised by my question, reported that 'boredom is a concept utterly, completely unknown' among the indigenous peoples he knew.

It is possible that anyone can learn to enjoy a slow pace of life. Used to my everyday busyness, I find it nearly impossible to sit down, relax, and read a book when on vacation. My motor just keeps running in high gear. Yet I once was able to spend enough time in such environs to happily pass entire days doing virtually nothing. It takes weeks or longer to get to that point, but once there it is extremely pleasant, and not at all boring. You can enjoy the simple pleasures of telling jokes about the people who can't just sit down and relax, for instance.

As well, *not* relaxing can get in the way of connection. When we used to do nothing, we didn't just do nothing alone; we very often did nothing together, or what is more usually known as hanging out. (Of course, there are limits to the fulfilments of idleness: life will start seeming pretty pointless if you don't get some meaningful activity in there somewhere.) There's no such thing as squeezing in 'quality time' with your loved ones. You just have to be together, do things together, in a natural, unscheduled, and unhurried way.

One reason for this, and a more general benefit of relaxing a bit, is that time opens up and you become more attentive and receptive to people and things around you, not locked in by the tunnel vision that hurry and stress tend to impose. Better able to appreciate things. As I noted earlier, life is in some ways shorter and more compressed when you don't relax enough.

An English nurse who worked with dying patients began tracking their regrets. Near the top of the list was this: 'I wish I hadn't worked so hard.' She writes:

> This came from every male patient that I nursed. They missed their children's youth and their partner's companionship. Women also spoke of this regret, but as most were from an older generation, many of the female patients had not been breadwinners. All of the men I nursed deeply regretted spending so much of their lives on the treadmill of a work existence.

There has lately been some controversy about whether people really tend to make very many serious mistakes about their lives. Among these male patients, at least, we appear to find a 100 per cent failure rate in how they handled some of the weightiest matters in their lives.

Slowing down the pace is one kind of relaxing. Another, though, is not blowing things out of proportion, getting more upset about troubles than they warrant. Not being needy, requiring the best of everything. Not dwelling on the negatives, feeding one's anger and anxieties. Shrugging or laughing off setbacks, choosing to see them as simply a part of the ride. There will always be setbacks.

Avoid debt

If you live in a modern economy, then money matters for happiness, and in a good life. I've been emphasizing how little it matters once you've achieved financial security. Here I want to stress how easy it is to lose that security. One of the wiser claims I have heard about happiness came from a very astute financial planner, whose line of work frequently makes him a family counsellor as well. In essence, he said that one of the biggest mistakes people make in the pursuit of happiness is taking on too much debt. In his words: 'most of the pain and suffering in today's economy is a result of too many consumers using too much debt...to buy too many things they never needed—and could not afford—in the first place'. We are the richest people who ever lived, and still we have trouble living within our means.

Debt is unfreedom: the more debt you've got, the less free you are to live as you want. Large debts make it hard to leave a job that makes you miserable, or gets you caught up in unethical practices. More than a few high-paid professionals, for instance, despise their jobs but owe so much in loans and mortgages in the sorts of houses that advertise 'success' that they're effectively trapped.

Home purchases pose special risks here, because we are vulnerable to 'focusing illusions' that make us exaggerate the importance of the differences between housing options. We tend to overlook crucial, shared features like non-leaky roofs and focus on the differences between our options, which may not be important at all. As psychologist Daniel Kahneman puts it, 'nothing in life is as important as you think it is when you're thinking about it'. In consequence, we put a lot of stock in trifling features like 'curb appeal', forgetting that we won't be spending much time sitting on the curb admiring our mini-mansion's many splendid (leaky) gables. Until, that is, the bank forecloses on us.

Make it come out even

The importance of being moral is pretty obvious, and I suspect you weren't seriously contemplating a life of rape and pillage. But we all slip up sometimes and do things we later feel bad about. Of all the things that give individuals pause when lying on their deathbeds, reflecting on their lives, probably the gravest regrets involve moral failures. Betraying a friend. Screwing up at raising your children. Not being there for someone in need. Showing too little forgiveness.

Simply advising people to 'be moral' seems too abstract to be very helpful. Let me frame the point, then, the way my great-grandmother Zada Tuteur put it, as described in one of my father's essays: *make it come out even*. This was, for her, the number one rule for living well.

From a philosopher's perspective this formula leaves much to be desired, as it is very inexact. But from a practical standpoint it seems usefully evocative.

The basic idea is to conclude your life with a favourable balance sheet. Many of us have an intuitive notion of a moral balance sheet (some cultures call it 'karma'): Have you taken care of your responsibilities? Or have you failed in your obligations, left behind a mess? Have you given enough back, or have you been a 'taker'? Are people glad to have had you in their lives?

Here's another way to think about it. Call it the 'conversation test'. Imagine sitting down with all those whose lives you've affected, including your children and grandchildren, and all those impacted by your lifestyle decisions. Would you be able to look them in the eye and honestly say that you treated them well enough, and with respect? That you were justified in the way you lived? You need not have an affirmative answer in every case—even the best of us fail to measure up at times. But you are not likely to feel you've made it come out even if you consistently fail the test. I suspect such questions will haunt many of my generation in coming decades, once the toll of today's wasteful habits has become all too apparent.

'Making it come out even' is a moral metric, not a measure of impacts. Perhaps some of the robber barons of the 19th century contributed more to the world than they took. Yet they may not have made it come out even if their gains were achieved through theft and brutality. Their moral balance sheets may decidedly have wound up in the red. On the flip side, extremely unlucky individuals may feel they've gotten a raw deal from society, and believe themselves entitled to even up the score by lashing out at others. But whether or not they received less than they gave to the world, this is not a plausible way to tilt the *moral* accounts in their favour. It is not a way to make it come out even. It simply makes things worse.

I had an uncle who was severely crippled for most of his life, requiring a great deal of care. He was a talented writer who earned some money publishing his work. But on the whole he may have received more, certainly in resources, than he was able to give. Yet by all accounts he made it come out even: he handled his situation with fortitude, wit, and a big heart, brought a great deal into many lives, and made them richer for it. Many people were glad, indeed felt privileged, to have him in their lives. And I suspect those who knew him would agree: he had a good life.

To make it come out even is to be able, when taking your dying breath, to honestly conclude that you've held up your end of things, done your part. And, on the whole, not regret the way you've treated others over the course of your life. We all have regrets about this or that thing we did wrong. But we can try to make amends, or do better elsewhere, so that, in the end, our balance sheets are in the black.

Conclusion

Summing up: Engage yourself with meaningful activities that interest you, but don't overdo it and forget to relax. Make time for the people you love. Keep a lid on your debts. And make it come out even.

And, I would add: make it easy for yourself to do these things by putting yourself in a context where they tend to come naturally. Surround yourself with good people who seem to you to have their priorities straight. Avoid careers that will put you in bad company. If most folks around you aren't doing a very good job of it, you'll find the going a lot harder.

Suppose, then, that you live as wisely as can reasonably be expected. Will you be happy? Maybe, but that's only partly in your control. But the chances are excellent that you'll have a life well-lived, and well worth living. A good life.

> Just being alive, having a wonderful family, good friends, watching the sunrise morning after morning—that's what makes me feel good. I think people take their lives for granted. Some just haven't hit that part of their lives where they stop and say, 'I am such a lucky person to have the life that I have'.
>
> Sgt. Michael A. DiRaimondo, in a letter home from Iraq, shortly before being killed in action

References and further reading

The chapter references are listed in their order of appearance within each chapter.

Chapter 1: A remarkable fact

Carol Graham, *Happiness Around the World: The Paradox of Happy Peasants and Miserable Millionaires* (Oxford University Press, 2009).

Table 1 is from W. Tov and E. Diener, 'Culture and Subjective Well-being', in S. Kitayama and D. Cohen, eds, *Handbook of Cultural Psychology* (Guilford Press, 2007), pp. 691–713.

'To date the best international study ...' *Gallup Global Wellbeing: The Behavioral Economics of GDP Growth* (2010). Accessed 12 December 2012 at <http://www.gallup.com/poll/126965/gallup-global-wellbeing.aspx>.

Daniel L. Everett, *Don't Sleep, There are Snakes: Life and Language in the Amazonian Jungle* (Random House, 2009).

Further reading

For an optimistic view of human life today, see Charles Kenny, *Getting Better: Why Global Development Is Succeeding—And How We Can Improve the World Even More* (Basic Books, 2011). On quality of life in small-scale societies, see Robert Biswas-Diener, Joar Vitterso, and Ed Diener, 'Most People are Pretty Happy, but There is Cultural Variation: The Inughuit, the Amish, and the Maasai', *The Journal of Happiness Studies*, 6/3 (2005), 205–26; Daniel

Everett, *Don't Sleep, There are Snakes: Life and Language in the Amazonian Jungle* (Random House, 2009); Robert B. Edgerton, *Sick Societies: Challenging the Myth of Primitive Harmony* (Free Press, 1992).

For brief reviews of how philosophers and other researchers think about happiness and well-being, see the *Stanford Encyclopedia of Philosophy* entries on these topics, at: <http://plato.stanford.edu/entries/happiness/>, and <http://plato.stanford.edu/entries/well-being/>. An accessible recent book is Sissela Bok, *Exploring Happiness: From Aristotle to Brain Science* (Yale University Press, 2010). For a highly readable history of Western thought about happiness in the 'well-being' sense, see Darrin M. McMahon, *Happiness: A History* (Atlantic Monthly Press, 2005).

For discussion of happiness as a social concern, see Richard Layard, *Happiness: Lessons from a New Science* (Penguin, 2005); Derek Bok, *The Politics of Happiness: What Government Can Learn from the New Research on Well-Being* (Princeton, 2010); Neil Thin, *Social Happiness: Evidence and Arguments for Collective Life Improvement* (Policy Press, 2012).

Chapter 2: What is happiness?

The quote is from an unpublished manuscript, excerpts of which appeared in 'Once Upon an Island', *The Gamut*, 33 (1991), 5–21.
'a lasting mark on your genes...': Marilyn J. Essex et al., 'Epigenetic Vestiges of Early Developmental Adversity: Childhood Stress Exposure and DNA Methylation in Adolescence', *Child Development* (2011), 1–18; S. G. Matthews and D. I. W. Phillips, 'Minireview: Transgenerational Inheritance of the Stress Response: A New Frontier in Stress Research', *Endocrinology*, 151/1 (2009), 7–13.

Further reading

This chapter is largely based on my *The Pursuit of Unhappiness: The Elusive Psychology of Well-Being* (Oxford University Press, 2008), which is less accessible but explores the issues in greater depth, including an extended argument against the hedonistic account of happiness. Some of the material in this chapter originally appeared there. A similar view of happiness appears in Matthieu Ricard's highly accessible *Happiness: A Guide to Developing Life's Most Important Skill* (Little, Brown and Co., 2006); the quoted passages appear on pp. 18–19. The notion of flow is discussed in Mihaly Csikszentmihalyi, *Flow: The Psychology of Optimum Experience* (Harper & Row, 1990).

The other two main scholarly books on happiness from contemporary philosophy are: L. W. Sumner, *Welfare, Happiness, and Ethics* (Oxford, 1996), 239; Fred Feldman, *What Is This Thing Called Happiness?* (Oxford, 2010). These three books span the three main views of happiness.

Chapter 3: Life satisfaction

The Moreese Bickham quotes hail from Kevin Sack, 'After 37 Years in Prison, Inmate Tastes Freedom', *The New York Times* (11 January 1996); Michelle Locke, 'Convict Returns to Different World After 37 Years', *The Seattle Times* (31 March 1996); Gene Mustain, 'He Savors Freedom After 38 Years', *New York Daily News* (14 January 1996). This example has also been used by Daniel Gilbert, *Stumbling on Happiness* (Knopf, 2006).

Ray Monk, *Ludwig Wittgenstein: The Duty of Genius* (Penguin, 1990), 579.

'...the 6-7 per cent of respondents...': Wolfgang Glatzer, 'Quality of Life in Advanced Industrialized Countries: The Case of West Germany', in F. Strack, M. Argyle, and N. Schwarz, eds, *Subjective Well-Being: An Interdisciplinary Perspective* (Pergamon Press, 1991), pp. 261–79.

Satisfaction in Calcutta: Robert Biswas-Diener and Ed Diener, 'Making the Best of a Bad Situation: Satisfaction in the Slums of Calcutta', *Social Indicators Research*, 55/3 (2001), 329–52.

'studies of Germans and Britons...': R. E. Lucas, 'Adaptation and the Set-Point Model of Subjective Well-Being: Does Happiness Change After Major Life Events?', *Current Directions in Psychological Science*, 16/2 (2007), 75–9.

The Egyptian quotes: Solava Ibrahim, 'A Comparative Analysis of Wellbeing Perceptions and Aspirations in Egypt and the UK', DSA 2012 Conference, 3 November 2012.

Indian health satisfaction: Amartya Sen, *The Idea of Justice* (Harvard University Press, 2009).

The dialysis and colostomy studies: Peter A. Ubel and George Loewenstein, 'Pain and Suffering Awards: They Shouldn't Be (Just) about Pain and Suffering', *The Journal of Legal Studies*, 37/s2 (2008), S195–S216.

Further reading

I discuss the problems for life satisfaction in much greater detail in *The Pursuit of Unhappiness*. An important defence of life satisfaction theories of happiness appears in L. W. Sumner, *Welfare, Happiness, and Ethics* (Oxford, 1996). Life satisfaction measures are defended in Ed Diener, Ronald Inglehart, and Louis Tay, 'Theory and Validity of Life Satisfaction Scales', *Social Indicators Research* (2012). The main critiques of life satisfaction covered in this chapter have only appeared in the last several years, so it is not yet clear how that debate will shape up over the long haul.

Chapter 4: Measuring happiness

Hemingway quote: Ernest Hemingway, *The Garden of Eden* (Simon and Schuster, 1995), p. 86.

'tend to track the sorts…': William Pavot, 'The Assessment of Subjective Well-Being: Successes and Shortfalls', in Michael Eid and Randy J. Larsen, eds, *The Science of Subjective Well-Being* (Guilford Press, 2008), pp. 124–40.

'…a 3:1 ratio of positive…': Barbara L. Fredrickson and Marcial F. Losada, 'Positive Affect and the Complex Dynamics of Human Flourishing', *American Psychologist*, 60/7 (2005), 678–86.

'A study of Germans…': Hermann Brandstatter, 'Emotions in Everyday Life Situations: Time Sampling of Subjective Experience', in F. Strack, M. Argyle, and N. Schwarz, eds, *Subjective Well-Being: An Interdisciplinary Perspective* (Pergamon Press, 1991), pp. 173–92.

'…oft-cited 1976 study of Americans': F. M. Andrews and S. B. Withey, *Social Indicators of Well-Being* (Plenum Press, 1976).

'…2007 Gallup poll…': 'Most Americans "Very Satisfied" with their Personal Lives', 31 December 2007, from Gallup, Inc.

World Values Survey: Ronald Inglehart and Hans-Dieter Klingemann, 'Genes, Culture, Democracy, and Happiness', in Ed Diener and Eunkook M. Suh, eds, *Culture and Subjective Well-Being* (MIT Press, 2000), pp. 165–83. More recent data, from 2005–8, are not much different, and can be viewed online at <http://www.worldvaluessurvey.org>.

'incarcerated...': Lauren E. Glaze, 'Correctional Populations in the United States, 2010' (US Department of Justice, Bureau of Justice Statistics, 2011), pp. 1–10.

'...rate of major depression': reported to be about 5 per cent in Maurice M. Ohayon, 'Epidemiology of Depression and its Treatment in the General Population', *Journal of Psychiatric Research*, 41/3–4 (2007), 207–13. See also Ronald C. Kessler et al., 'Impairment in Pure and Comorbid Generalized Anxiety Disorder and Major Depression at 12 Months in Two National Surveys', *American Journal of Psychiatry*, 156/12 (1999), 1915–23.

'...either major depression or a generalized anxiety disorder': Ronald C. Kessler et al., 'Prevalence, Severity, and Comorbidity of 12-Month DSM-IV Disorders in the National Comorbidity Survey Replication', *Archives of General Psychiatry*, 62/6 (2005), 617–27. For further discussion, see my *The Pursuit of Unhappiness: The Elusive Psychology of Well-Being* (Oxford University Press, 2008).

'took antidepressants...': 'F.D.A. Expands Suicide Warning on Drugs', *The New York Times*, 3 May 2007.

'report feeling sad...': See e.g. *The Gallup-Healthways Monthly U.S. Well-Being Report*, December 2011; 'Americans' Emotional Health Reaches Four-Year High' (10 May 2012). Both available online at <http://www.gallup.com>.

'extreme levels of stress': *Stress in America* (The American Psychological Association, 2007).

Chronic insomnia: Nancy J. Pearson, Laura Lee Johnson, and Richard L. Nahin, 'Insomnia, Trouble Sleeping, and Complementary and Alternative Medicine: Analysis of the 2002 National Health Interview Survey Data', *Archives of Internal Medicine*, 166 (18 September 2006), 1775–82.

Confidants: Miller McPherson, Matthew E. Brashears, and Lynn Smith-Lovin, 'Social Isolation in America: Changes in Core Discussion Networks over Two Decades', *American Sociological Review*, 71/3 (2006), 353–75.

'feel sufficiently isolated...': John T. Cacioppo and William Patrick, *Loneliness: Human Nature and the Need for Social Connection* (W. W. Norton, 2009).

'...attempted suicide': David J. Drum et al., 'New Data on the Nature of Suicidal Crises in College Students: Shifting the Paradigm',

Professional Psychology: Research and Practice, 40/3 (2009), 213–22.

'A study of tenth grade girls…': Suniya S. Luthar and Bronwyn E. Becker, 'Privileged but Pressured? A Study of Affluent Youth', *Child Development*, 73/5 (2002), 1593–610.

'self-injury': Elizabeth E. Lloyd-Richardson et al., 'Characteristics and Functions of Non-suicidal Self-injury in a Community Sample of Adolescents', *Psychological Medicine*, 37/08 (2007), 1183; Janis Whitlock, John Eckenrode, and Daniel Silverman, 'Self-injurious Behaviors in a College Population', *Pediatrics*, 117 (2006), 1939–48.

'…make themselves vomit': Yiing Mei Liou et al., 'Prevalence and Correlates of Self-induced Vomiting as Weight-control Strategy among Adolescents in Taiwan', *Journal of Clinical Nursing*, 21/1–2 (2011), 11–20.

'positive illusions': Shelley E. Taylor and Jonathan D. Brown, 'Illusion and Well-Being: A Social-Psychological Perspective on Mental Health', *Psychological Bulletin*, 103 (1988), 193–210.

Further reading

An excellent survey of the current state of happiness research, including applications to policy, is John Helliwell, Richard Layard, and Jeffrey Sachs, *World Happiness Report* (The Earth Institute, 2012), pp. 1–158, available as a free download.

Accessible books surveying the science of happiness include Daniel Nettle, *Happiness: The Science Behind Your Smile* (Oxford, 2005); Richard Layard, *Happiness: Lessons from a New Science* (Penguin, 2005); Ed Diener and Robert Biswas-Diener, *Happiness: Unlocking the Mysteries of Psychological Wealth* (Blackwell, 2008).

Most of the research cited in this chapter is discussed in my *The Pursuit of Unhappiness: The Elusive Psychology of Well-Being*, from which some passages were adapted.

Chapter 5: The sources of happiness

'In one paper on the heritability…': David Lykken and Auke Tellegen, 'Happiness is a Stochastic Phenomenon', *Psychological Science*, 7/3 (1996), 186–9.

'men in the Netherlands…': R. W. Fogel, 'Changes in the Disparities in Chronic Diseases During the Course of the 20th Century',

Perspectives in Biology and Medicine, 48/1 Supplement (2005), S150–S65.

Robert Kenny quote: Graeme Wood, 'The Secret Fears of the Super-Rich', *The Atlantic Monthly* (April 2011).

'...Department of Justice reports...': David Finkelhor et al., 'Nonfamily Abducted Children: National Estimates and Characteristics', US Department of Justice Office of Juvenile Justice and Delinquency Prevention, *NISMART* (October 2002).

'horses...': D. M. Bixby-Hammett, 'Accidents in Equestrian Sports', *American Family Physician*, 36/3 (1987), 209–14. Cited in Raymond A. Cripps, 'Horse-related Injury in Australia', *Australian Injury Prevention Bulletin*, 24 (2000).

Bees, wasps, and hornets: R. L. Langley, 'Animal-related Fatalities in the United States—An Update', *Wilderness & Environmental Medicine*, 16/2 (2005), 67–74.

The falling and flu figures appear in D. Ropeik, *How Risky Is It, Really? Why Our Fears Don't Always Match the Facts* (McGraw-Hill, 2010).

The studies involving Ricard are discussed in Robert W. Levenson, Paul Ekman, and Matthieu Ricard, 'Meditation and the Startle Response: A Case Study', *Emotion*, 12/3 (2012), 650–58. The body temperature findings are summarized in W. J. Cromie, 'Meditation Changes Temperatures', *Harvard Gazette* (18 April 2002).

'people who care more about others...': a good review appears in Sonia Lyubomirsky, *The How of Happiness* (Penguin, 2007).

'only dancing...': Michael Argyle, 'Causes and Correlates of Happiness', in Daniel Kahneman, Ed Diener, and Norbert Schwarz, eds, *Well-Being: The Foundations of Hedonic Psychology* (Russell Sage Foundation, 1999), pp. 3–25.

'spending money on others...': E. W. Dunn, L. B. Aknin, and M. I. Norton, 'Spending Money on Others Promotes Happiness', *Science*, 319/5870 (2008), 1687–88.

'materialistic values...': Tim Kasser, *The High Price of Materialism* (MIT Press, 2002). The distinction between intrinsic and extrinsic motivation is somewhat problematic, but the general point here should be clear enough.

Quote: Tepilit Ole Saitoti, *The Worlds of a Maasai Warrior: An Autobiography* (University of California Press, 1986), p. 82.

Control: for an accessible discussion with references, see Daniel Gilbert, *Stumbling on Happiness* (Knopf, 2006).

'the costs of choice...': Barry Schwartz, 'Self-Determination: The
   Tyranny of Freedom', *American Psychologist*, 55/1 (2000), 79–88;
   The Paradox of Choice (HarperCollins, 2004).
'Parts of Southeast Asia': Robert Wolff, *What It Is to Be Human*
   (Periwinkle Press, 1994).
'most recent World Values Survey': R. Inglehart et al., 'Development,
   Freedom, and Rising Happiness: A Global Perspective (1981–2007)',
   Perspectives on Psychological Science, 3/4 (2008), 264–85.
'one of the better predictors of happiness and satisfaction': One recent
   paper claims it to be the *strongest* predictor: Paolo Verme,
   'Happiness, Freedom and Control', *Journal of Economic Behavior
   & Organization*, 71/2 (2009), 146–61.
'study of highly happy individuals...': Ed Diener and Martin E.
   Seligman, 'Very Happy People', *Psychological Science*, 13/1 (2002),
   81–84.
'Psychologists Ed Diener and Robert Biswas-Diener...': E. Diener and
   R. Biswas-Diener, *Happiness: Unlocking the Mysteries of
   Psychological Wealth* (Blackwell, 2008).
'measures of trust correlate...': John F. Helliwell and Robert Putnam,
   'The Social Context of Well-Being', *Philosophical Transactions of
   the Royal Society*, 359/1449 (2004), 1435–46.
'Studies that track...': E. Diener and R. Biswas-Diener, *Happiness:
   Unlocking the Mysteries of Psychological Wealth* (Blackwell, 2008).
'Watching television...': Daniel Kahneman et al., 'A Survey Method
   for Characterizing Daily Life Experience: The Day Reconstruction
   Method', *Science*, 306/5702 (December 2004), 1776–80.
'The state of flow...': Mihaly Csikszentmihalyi, *Flow: The Psychology
   of Optimum Experience* (Harper & Row, 1990).
'...as worthwhile or meaningful': See the papers collected in Alan
   Waterman, ed., *The Best Within Us: Positive Psychology
   Perspectives on Eudaimonic Functioning* (American Psychological
   Association, 2013). Most research focuses on a general sense
   of meaning or purpose in life rather than the experienced
   meaningfulness of one's activities, so while the benefits of
   meaningful activity are widely affirmed, the evidence is largely
   indirect. A promising new approach appears in Mathew P. White
   and Paul Dolan, 'Accounting for the Richness of Daily Activities',
   Psychological Science, 20/8 (2009), 1000–08. Note that meaningful
   activity need not be pleasant at the time to contribute to happiness
   over the long haul.

'nature has a remarkably powerful impact...': for references, see my
'Central Park: Nature, Context, and Human Wellbeing',
International Journal of Wellbeing, 1/2 (2011), 235–54. A highly
readable discussion is Richard Louv, *Last Child in the Woods:
Saving our Children from Nature-deficit Disorder* (Algonquin
Books, 2008).

'James Martin': James Martin, *In Good Company: The Fast Track
from the Corporate World to Poverty, Chastity, and Obedience*
(Sheed & Ward, 2000).

'until about $75,000': D. Kahneman and A. Deaton, 'High Income
Improves Evaluation of Life but Not Emotional Well-being',
Proceedings of the National Academy of Sciences, 107/38 (2010),
16489–93.

'Monterrey, Mexico...': Nicole Fuentes and Mariano Rojas, 'Economic
Theory and Subjective Well-being: Mexico', *Social Indicators
Research*, 53/3 (2001), 289–314.

'Looking worldwide...': Ed Diener et al., 'Wealth and Happiness
across the World: Material Prosperity Predicts Life Evaluation,
Whereas Psychosocial Prosperity Predicts Positive Feeling', *Journal
of Personality and Social Psychology*, 99/1 (2010), 52–61.

'Once you control...': John Helliwell, Richard Layard, and Jeffrey
Sachs, 'World Happiness Report' (The Earth Institute, 2012),
pp. 1–158.

'building a better society...': see, for example, Richard Layard,
Happiness: Lessons from a New Science (Penguin, 2005); Derek
Bok, *The Politics of Happiness: What Government Can Learn from
the New Research on Well-Being* (Princeton, 2010).

Further reading

Accessible discussions of the sources of happiness can be found in the
references recommended in Chapter 4. Good sources on methods
for becoming happier include Mihaly Csikszentmihalyi, *Flow:
The Psychology of Optimum Experience* (Harper & Row, 1990);
Martin Seligman, *Flourish: A Visionary New Understanding of
Happiness and Well-being* (Simon & Schuster, 2011); Sonia
Lyubomirsky, *The How of Happiness* (Penguin, 2007); Daniel
Gilbert, *Stumbling on Happiness* (Knopf, 2006); and Matthieu
Ricard, *Happiness: A Guide to Developing Life's Most Important
Skill* (Little, Brown and Co., 2006).

For a discussion of the 'basic needs' view on which the SOARS model is partly based, including references on autonomy, relationships, and skilled activity (competence), see Richard M. Ryan, Randall Curren, and Edward L. Deci, 'What Humans Need: Flourishing in Aristotelian Philosophy and Self-Determination Theory', in Alan Waterman, ed., *The Best Within Us: Positive Psychology Perspectives on Eudaimonia* (American Psychological Association, 2013).

Chapter 6: Beyond happiness: well-being

'Nozick first proposed...': Robert Nozick, *Anarchy, State, and Utopia* (Basic Books, 1974).

'study spanning ten countries...': Christopher Y. Olivola et al., 'Reality Does Not Bite' (Unpublished manuscript).

'grass-counter...': John Rawls, *A Theory of Justice* (Harvard University Press, 1971).

'eudaimonic psychology': for a review, see Alan Waterman, ed., *The Best Within Us: Positive Psychology Perspectives on Eudaimonic Functioning* (American Psychological Association, 2013).

'Sumner may have pointed...': L. W. Sumner, *Welfare, Happiness, and Ethics* (Oxford, 1996).

Further reading

The philosophical literature on well-being is tough going for the non-academic reader. The best and most accessible brief overview is the well-being entry in the *Stanford Encyclopedia of Philosophy* at: <http://plato.stanford.edu/entries/well-being/>.

Probably the most accessible book offering a comprehensive discussion of well-being, and defending the authentic happiness view, is L. W. Sumner, *Welfare, Happiness, and Ethics* (Oxford, 1996), p. 239. A recent defence of hedonism appears in Roger Crisp, *Reasons and the Good* (Oxford, 2006). For an Aristotelian perspective, see Richard Kraut, *What is Good and Why* (Harvard University Press, 2007). A sophisticated version of the desire theory is defended in James Griffin, *Well-Being: Its Meaning, Measurement, and Moral Importance* (Clarendon Press, 1986). For a survey of ancient thinking about well-being (using the word 'happiness'), see Julia Annas, *The Morality of Happiness* (Oxford, 1993).

Chapter 7: Getting outside oneself: virtue and meaning

'parents seem not to be happier...': For an accessible review, see
  Daniel Gilbert, *Stumbling on Happiness* (Knopf, 2006).
'some researchers claim...': S. K. Nelson et al., 'In Defense of
  Parenthood: Children Are Associated With More Joy Than Misery',
  Psychological Science, 24/1 (2013), 3–10.
'France found it to be...': Alan Krueger et al., 'Time Use and
  Subjective Well-Being in France and the US', *Social Indicators
  Research*, 93 (2009), 7–18.
'having merit or worth...': My discussion of meaning is partly based
  on Stephen Darwall's 'Aristotelian Thesis' about well-being,
  discussed in *Welfare and Rational Care* (Princeton University
  Press, 2002).
'making our lives more meaningful...': Mathew P. White and Paul
  Dolan, 'Accounting for the Richness of Daily Activities',
  Psychological Science, 20/8 (2009), 1000–08. Dolan is developing
  a version of the idea that reward or meaning is a special kind of
  valuable experience.
'Susan Wolf...': Susan R. Wolf, *Meaning in Life and Why It Matters*
  (Princeton University Press, 2010).
'fruits of your labor...': Matthew B. Crawford, *Shop Class as Soulcraft:
  An Inquiry Into the Value of Work* (Penguin Press, 2009).

Further reading

An accessible and influential discussion of meaning appears in
  S. R. Wolf, *Meaning in Life and Why It Matters* (Princeton
  University Press, 2010). My work in this chapter has especially
  been influenced by Stephen Darwall, *Welfare and Rational Care*
  (Princeton University Press, 2002).

Chapter 8: A good life

I borrow the term 'justified affirmation' from Lynne McFall,
  Happiness (Peter Lang, 1989).
'negativity bias...': Roy F. Baumeister et al., 'Bad is Stronger than
  Good', *Review of General Psychology*, 5 (2001), 323–70.
'Someday, someday...': Sherry Turkle, 'The Flight from Conversation',
  The New York Times (21 April 2012).

'major employment study...': A. P. Carnevale, B. Cheah, and J. Strohl, 'Hard Times, College Majors, Unemployment and Earnings: Not All College Degrees Are Created Equal' (Georgetown University Center on Education and the Workforce, 2012).

'Laurie says Ravioli...': Adam Gopnik, 'Bumping Into Mr Ravioli', *The New Yorker* (30 September 2002), 80–84.

'Mexican businessman...': 'Jorge Sosa, Man of Two Cultures', <yucatanliving.com>, accessed 4 January 2013.

'An English nurse...': Susie Steiner, 'Top Five Regrets of the Dying', *The Guardian* (1 February 2012).

'financial planner...': Robert J. Sullivan, CFP, Co-Founder, Sullivan & Serwitz.

'focusing illusions': D. Kahneman, *Thinking, Fast and Slow* (Farrar, Straus and Giroux, 2011).

'most common regrets...': Daniel Gilbert, *Stumbling on Happiness* (Knopf, 2006).

'one of my father's essays: Ron Haybron, 'Making It Come Out Even', based on talks for the Hemlock and Unitarian Societies (1994).

'Sgt. Michael A. DiRaimondo...': 'The Things They Wrote', *The New York Times* (24 March 2004).

Further reading

For a accessible discussion of the good life, see Thomas Hurka, *The Best Things in Life: A Guide to What Really Matters* (Oxford University Press, 2010). For a more advanced but clearly written discussion, see Valerie Tiberius, *The Reflective Life: Living Wisely With Our Limits* (Oxford, 2008).

Index

Index

virtue and 62–3, 92–7, 106–7;
see also virtue
happy slaves 86, 87
happy, feeling 18, 19–20
Haybron, Ron 14, 18
health 7, 17, 29, 39, 44, 65, 72, 106
hedonic balance 25; *see also*
pleasant vs. unpleasant
experience
hedonic good 36; *see also* pleasant
vs. unpleasant experience
hedonic treadmill 53–4
hedonism, *see* happiness, hedonistic
theories of, and well-being,
hedonistic theories of
Helliwell, John 134, 136, 137
helping others, *see* caring for
others; virtue
Hemingway, Ernest 42, 48, 115
heritability, *see* happiness,
genes and
Hobbes, Thomas 96, 103–4
homeless 4
homosexuality 87
honesty 62, 71, 92–3, 105, 116
human enhancement 87
human nature 65, 70, 82, 90, 98
humour 61; *see also* laughter
Hunter-gatherers 3, 5–6, 7, 66, 67,
122; *see also* Pirahãs
Hurka, Thomas 140
hurry, *see* busyness

I

identity 57, 67, 88
idleness 122
immorality 93, 95–7
impoverishment 20, 25, 79–80, 83,
85, 86
incarceration rates in the United
States 48
income 47, 73, 74, 109, 119–20;
see also money
India, *see* Calcutta

individualism 66–7
insomnia 49
integrity 62, 98
Inughuit 3–4
Italy 45

J

joy 14, 17, 18, 19, 20, 23, 62, 100,
101, 104
justice 82, 93

K

Kahneman, Daniel 124, 135, 136,
137, 140
Kenny, Charles 1
Kenny, Robert 56
King, Martin Luther 101, 112
knowledge 86, 102
Kolkata, *see* Calcutta
Kraut, Richard 138

L

Latin America 64, 67
laughter 5, 16, 17, 18, 20, 42, 44,
107, 123
Layard, Richard 130, 134, 137
leisure 62, 104; *see also* activity;
television; video games
life expectancy 1–2, 5, 7
life satisfaction 3, 4, 5, 9, 11, 12, 30,
31–41, 44, 45, 74, 75, 114;
see also happiness, life
satisfaction theories of
defined 11–12, 32, 35–6
importance of 36–41
measures of 36, 40–1, 44,
45, 74
liking vs. appreciating 98–9
Lincoln, Abraham 112
living well 97, 111, 116, 125;
see also virtue
loneliness 49, 91

Index

145

Happiness

SOCIAL MEDIA
Very Short Introduction

Join our community
www.oup.com/vsi

- Join us online at the official Very Short Introductions
  Facebook page.
- Access the thoughts and musings of our authors with our
  online **blog**.
- Sign up for our monthly **e-newsletter** to receive information
  on all new titles publishing that month.
- Browse the full range of Very Short Introductions online.
- Read **extracts** from the Introductions for free.
- Visit our library of **Reading Guides**. These guides, written by our
  expert authors will help you to question again, why you think
  what you think.
- If you are a teacher or lecturer you can order inspection
  copies quickly and simply via our website.

Visit the Very Short Introductions website to access all this and
more for free.
www.oup.com/vsi